Wherever

forty devotions to encourage and inspire

Wherever: forty devotions to encourage and inspire
Published (2016) by Village Creek Bible Camp

All individual contributors maintain individual ownership and rights to their written and art contributions published in this book. Each has granted permission for printing of these materials in this collection.
ISBN: 1530835798
ISBN-13: 978-1530835799

Compiled and edited by Stacy A. Bender
Cover art and design by Lori R. Hetteen – Used with permission

Scripture quotations marked (ERV) are taken from the HOLY BIBLE: EASY-TO-READ VERSION © 2014 by Bible League International and used by permission.

Scripture quotations marked (ESV) are from the ESV® Bible (The Holy Bible, English Standard Version®), copyright © 2001 by Crossway, a publishing ministry of Good News Publishers. Used by permission. All rights reserved.

Scripture quotations marked (HCSB)®, are taken from the Holman Christian Standard Bible®, Copyright © 1999, 2000, 2002, 2003, 2009 by Holman Bible Publishers. Used by permission. HCSB® is a federally registered trademark of Holman Bible Publishers.

Scripture quotations marked (NASB) are from from the New American Standard Bible®, Copyright © 1960, 1962, 1963, 1968, 1971, 1972, 1973, 1975, 1977, 1995 by The Lockman Foundation. Used by permission. (www.Lockman.org)

Scripture quotations marked (NIV) are taken from the Holy Bible, NEW INTERNATIONAL VERSION®, NIV® Copyright © 1973, 1978, 1984, 2011 by Biblica, Inc.®Used by permission. All rights reserved worldwide.

Scripture quotations marked (NLT) are taken from the HOLY BIBLE, New Living Translation, copyright ©1996, 2004, 2007, 2013 by Tyndale House Foundation. Used by permission of Tyndale House Publishers, Inc., Carol Stream, Illinois 60188. All rights reserved.

Scripture taken from The Voice™. Copyright © 2008 by Ecclesia Bible Society. Used by permission. All rights reserved.

Editor's Acknowledgements

We give all honor and glory to God, our Creator, Redeemer, and Sustainer. We thank Him for all of His guidance on this project and know that He will use it as He sees fit.

The contributing authors of this book are a talented bunch. We welcomed some new authors this year, and it was so fun to see them join in the project. No one involved in this project benefits financially, and their giving of their time and talent is a profound gift. Readers can find information about individual authors at the end of the book. Thank you to each author!

Lori Hetteen provided the cover art, multiple graphics inside the book, and was a sounding board for most things related to layout, design, and art. Her talent is an integral part of this project as her art provided inspiration for the authors before they started to write. More information about Lori and where to find her artwork can be found at the end of the book. Thank you!

Jen Woyke, author of the "hymn reflections" at the beginning of each section, provided support, ideas, and assistance throughout most stages of this project. Thank you!

Anita Pelzer provided critical editing eyes - a "first edit" for all of those tricky punctuation and grammar issues. Thank you!

In addition to writing an entry this year, Sue Lyford provided all of the business-related support as well as the Village Creek Bible Camp portions of the marketing through Facebook, Twitter, the camp website, and mass emails. Thank you!

Tom and Camie Treptau, as executive director and co-director of Village Creek Bible Camp, provided initial approval of, direction for, and support throughout the project. Thank you!

All net proceeds from this project directly support the ministries at Village Creek Bible Camp (VCBC) located in Lansing, Iowa. The camp provides year-round camps, retreats, and other programming for all ages.

You will find more information about Village Creek Bible Camp at the end of this book.

If you use this devotion over the summer, consider using the prayer guide on page 113 to pray for VCBC or another Christian camp – perhaps one that you support or live near.

Introduction

When Camie Treptau, co-director of Village Creek Bible Camp, and I hatched the plan in March 2015 to publish a devotion book written by authors associated with the camp, we had no idea the impact it would have. As the year progressed, we have seen so many blessings come from *Anchored*.

As I started to put together the team for this year's project, a nagging voice said, "It can't be as good as last year's book." Most of me believed that voice. I loved last year's art work, and I loved the way that the hymns tied to the sections. *Anchored* was a project that far exceeded my expectations; how could *Wherever* do the same thing?

I need to admit that I was not initially thrilled when Camie told me this year's theme. It simply did not catch me like *Anchored* had. Who can argue with God being their anchor? I wasn't sure how *Wherever* could have the same impact. It seemed a bit abstract to me.

That all changed when Lori sent me the draft of the cover art. It immediately gave life to this year's theme. The "mini scenes" in each of the letters give concrete examples of where God meets us.

Whether we are lost in a storm of suffering or wandering in our personal wilderness, the idea of *Wherever* applies to us. Each person walks his or her story on the path of suffering, wandering, community, or joy. God finds us there, meets our needs, and brings us into closer relationship with Him in, despite, and through our paths. His mysterious redemptive work is always happening around us regardless of whether we see Him or not, but He assures us that He is there in the midst of it all.

Wherever you are today, know that God – through the saving blood of Jesus – desires to meet you and know you.

-sb, editor

7 - Suffering

My life flows on in endless song;
Above earth's lamentation
I hear the sweet though far off hymn
That hails a new creation:
Through all the tumult and the strife
I hear the music ringing;
It finds an echo in my soul—
How can I keep from singing?

What though my joys and comforts die?
The Lord my Savior liveth;
What though the darkness gather round!
Songs in the night He giveth:
No storm can shake my inmost calm
While to that refuge clinging;
Since Christ is Lord of Heav'n and earth,
How can I keep from singing?

I lift mine eyes; the cloud grows thin;
I see the blue above it;
And day by day this pathway smoothes
Since first I learned to love it:
The peace of Christ makes fresh my heart,
A fountain ever springing:
All things are mine since I am His—
How can I keep from singing?[1]

Robert Lowry

Hymn Reflection: Suffering
by Jen Woyke

I love hymns. There is something very powerful about singing praise with the same words God's people used 50 years, or 150 years, or 1000 years ago. This hymn in particular is one of my favorites. I think the poetic style is beautiful but that's not why I love it. I love it because verse to verse it tells the story of God walking with us through each day, through each struggle, through each challenge. It reminds me that things are broken in our world but the peace of Christ can renew me.

Robert Lowry wrote *How Can I Keep From Singing?* as a young pastor in New York City during the dark days leading up to the Civil War. Uncertainty and the expectation of certain war hung in the air. It was into that circumstance he penned these words. Words that remind us that wherever we are, whatever suffering we find ourselves in the midst of, God is there. A God who gives songs in the night to comfort, a God who provides a sure anchor we can cling to, a God who promises a new creation, a God who makes fresh our hearts in any, and every, circumstance. Because of that, Lowry's soul could not keep from singing!

Life can be really hard sometimes, and things can look very bleak. But you serve a God who gives peace, who will renew your heart, who desires to walk with you through hard stuff. Let your soul sing today, as you are inspired by the same truth, the same God, who inspired Robert Lowry 150 years ago.

June 29, 2024

10 - Suffering

The Blessed Life
by Pastor Kerry L. Bender

Psalm 32:1 - A Psalm of King David
Blessed is the one whose transgression is forgiven, whose sin is covered.

In first grade, I cheated on a spelling quiz. I carried this secret with me until graduation day.

When my first grade teacher Mrs. Rutschke (ironically, I am not sure that is the correct spelling) came through the receiving line, I blurted out the truth. I just couldn't take it anymore – and I had my diploma safely in hand.

This episode and countless others since, unfortunately, have taught me an important but painful truth; the vast majority of suffering in my life is self-inflicted.

Oh, I don't believe in a God who sits above us like an overgrown adolescent watching us, waiting for us to screw up so that he can crush us with his thumb. No, but I do believe that my sin has consequences, and those consequences cause suffering and pain in my life and far too often in the lives of others.

Guilt. Shame. Regret. Isolation! Is there a deeper suffering than the secret sin held deep inside the mind, the conscience, the soul? A suffering that will not relent. That weighs heavy upon us day and night. That eats away at us from the inside out.

King David knew this suffering. He sinned. He hid that sin. And he SUFFERED. Until he confessed and discovered that the blessed life isn't the perfect life but the forgiven life.

When my son Siah was 5 years old he sat on our kitchen floor and pointed to two blue squares in the linoleum separated by a grey line.

He said, "Daddy, if this blue square is 'good' and this blue square is 'bad,' where am I on the line?"

His question is a profound one, not because of what he was asking explicitly, but because of the question that was implied, unspoken, but crying out from his very core.

I sat down on the floor, put him in my lap, hugged him, and told him how much I loved him. That's what he wanted to know.

God does not care where you are on the grey line between "good" and "bad." He sent his son, Jesus Christ, while we were yet sinners, so we can have forgiveness of sin, freedom from guilt, and the promise of life everlasting. This puts an end to our greatest suffering, brings light to our darkest hour, and heals to our deepest wounds.

If God can redeem my greatest suffering – my sin, my guilt, my shame – then I trust that he can redeem all of my suffering – self-inflicted or otherwise.

Heavenly Father, I confess my sin to you, and I thank you for your unrelenting love calling me to repentance. Thank you for redeeming my greatest suffering – my sin, my guilt, my shame. I trust that in your own time, and in your own way, you will bring about the redemption of all my suffering. In Christ's powerful name, Amen.

Aug. 22, 2016
March 11, 2017
June 26, 2024

Light and Momentary Troubles
by R. Lee Boleyn

2 Corinthians 4:17-18 (NIV)

For our light and momentary troubles are achieving for us
an eternal glory that far outweighs them all.
So we fix our eyes not on what is seen, but on what is unseen.
For what is seen is temporary, but what is unseen is eternal.

When I was about two years old, I contracted polio and was, I am told, very sick. God's grace and the prayers of his people resulted in healing with no apparent or obvious side effects. However, through the years, I have regularly experienced pain and discomfort with seemingly no cause. I have often felt, and have expressed to others, that I "suffer" from post-polio syndrome. More recently, I was diagnosed with melanoma skin cancer and because of an inadequate biopsy procedure, a more complete sentinel node biopsy was performed to make sure the cancer had not spread. Thankfully, it had not! However, the result of that more extensive surgical procedure resulted in numbness and pain in the tissue of my left ear and the left side of my face and neck...daily reminders of physical "suffering".

As so many of you, I have "suffered" the pain of loss and grief with the death of both parents, a younger sister and other extended family members. Suffering is a normal part of life but I don't believe God's original plan was for his creation to suffer. One of the consequences of Adam and Eve's disobedience was suffering (Genesis 3:16-19).

Some of the suffering we experience is the result of poor choices and some the result of our committed Christian lifestyle, but much of the suffering we experience is simply the result of living in a fallen world. However we look at suffering, it is unavoidable. So how do we respond in times of suffering? The Apostle Paul tells us in our scripture text first to understand that our sufferings are insignificant in comparison to the glory we are going to experience in God's eternal presence. Secondly, in some mysterious way, suffering is one of the tools God uses to shape our character. Paul's personal testimony of suffering in these and previous verses (and in his other letters) reminds me that my focus should not be on myself but should be on God and his provision... *"fix (your) eyes not on what is seen, but on what is unseen."*

What a challenge, and so counter-intuitive, because often my first response to suffering is to say or think, *"Poor me. God, why are you doing this to me?"* Or, my response is to look solely to human advice and manmade solutions to find relief or release from suffering when instead I should be asking God for his strength, turning my spiritual eyes to his power and grace which is sufficient for me (2 Cor. 12:9).

My daily numbness and discomfort stemming from a surgical procedure is also a daily reminder to focus in the right place. Other types of suffering I may experience are light and momentary troubles in light of eternity. The challenge is to believe it and then act on that belief by staying focused on God.

Dear Jesus, help me to constantly look to you for sufficiency, and in times of suffering give me the desire and strength to fix my eyes on what is unseen and eternal. Thank you for the promise of your eternal glory which is already present in my life. Amen.

Aug 23, 2016
March 21, 2017

Sept 21, 2017
June 28, 2024

How to Survive the Wilderness
by Joel Detlefsen

Luke 4:1b (ESV)
...and [Jesus] *was led by the Spirit in the wilderness...*

Last summer I was on a road trip in the high desert of Nevada. It was a wasteland of sand, rocks, and little vegetation. We stopped at a rest station and a wave of immense heat blew in my face as I got out of the car. Thank God for cars and air conditioning!

The wilderness in Israel is similar to the Nevada desert except maybe even more harsh. It's like a desert, but with less sand and more things that can hurt and kill you – and that doesn't include the unbearable heat or lack of food and water. Put simply, the wilderness is a miserable place to be, full of difficulty, hardship, and pain.

In Luke 4, Jesus had just been baptized and was *"led by the Spirit into the wilderness."* It goes without saying that while Jesus was in the wilderness he was miserable. No food, little water, barely enough to be able to stay alive. And all the while, the devil was pestering him and making his life – and his walk with God – all the more difficult. Like Jesus, we all either have been, or will be at one point or another, "in the wilderness." That is, we will go through hard times that will test our faith and make our walk with God difficult. During those times, we can learn from Jesus by following his example for how he survived in the wilderness.

---

15 - Suffering

First, Luke 4:1 says that Jesus *"was led by the Spirit in the wilderness…"* Jesus didn't stumble into the wilderness by accident. It wasn't by mistake that he experienced this time of difficulty and suffering. Rather, it was God who led him there. Jesus' "wilderness moment" was a creation of God's design that existed for God's purposes (see Hebrews 4:15 for God's purpose in Jesus' "wilderness moment"). God had his own intentions for Jesus' suffering; it wasn't to hurt him or to make him miserable.

Second, Luke 4:1 does *not* say that the Spirit led Jesus into the wilderness…and then left him. No. Rather, *the Spirit stayed with Jesus the entire time he was in the wilderness,* for forty days. When you are in the wilderness, remember that God's Spirit has not left you but is with you, walking the path of hard times right alongside you. Trust in his guidance. (See Exodus 3:11-12, Joshua 1:9, and Psalm 23:4 for more about how God promises to be with us in hard times.)

Finally, when Jesus was in the wilderness, he immersed himself in God's word. By going to God's word in the time of his difficulty, Jesus fought off temptation and doubt and reminded himself of God's goodness and provision. In the same way, and for the same reasons, we can and should go to the word of God in our times of suffering and difficulty.

Is it fun to be in the wilderness? No, but God has led us there for a reason. When we follow Jesus' example of how to survive the wilderness we can come out of it trusting God more and looking more and more like Jesus.

Jesus – thank you for going to the wilderness and for helping me when I am in the wilderness. Be with me, teach me, and lead me through all of my days.

Where Will Your Suffering Take You?
by Abigail Dodds

Hebrews 4:14-16 (ESV)
Since then we have a great high priest who has passed through the heavens, Jesus, the Son of God, let us hold fast our confession. For we do not have a high priest who is unable to sympathize with our weaknesses, but one who in every respect has been tempted as we are, yet without sin. Let us then with confidence draw near to the throne of grace, that we may receive mercy and find grace to help in time of need.

Our trials can produce all kinds of results in our lives. Some are beautiful and some are ugly.

I've been mulling over one of the beautiful things that Jesus' suffering did in his life. Because of his own suffering, we have a high priest who IS able to sympathize. His sympathy was secured by his trials and temptations. Do our trials and temptations secure our sympathy for others? Do our trials lead us to the throne of grace, pushing back our tendency toward disobedience and ushering mercy and help in our time of need?

During hard times, the temptations to sin are great. One way that sin tries to take hold is by telling us our suffering is too great to walk through without being angry or bitter. Sin tells us that our trial is so unique and difficult that no one else can really understand it or help us through it. This is the path to bitterness. Bitterness can never be validated enough, it is a vacuous hole of irritation at everyone else for not experiencing the suffering I've experienced. Bitterness is a martyr. Bitterness can only be satiated at the cross of Jesus Christ, with the acknowledgement that he has borne it all for us, and there is none to rival his pain.

Forgetfulness is another ugly road suffering can take us down. We come through some hard thing and at the end we're done. We have filled our suffering quotient and have done what we had to do to get through it. It's behind us now. We'd rather not be around the people still stuck in some awful situation. Or, if we are around them, we conveniently offer the "to-dos" of how to get through it. Buck up. We've been there, and we're over it. Everyone else should get over it too. Forgetfulness as a means of avoiding is unhelpful at best and untrue at worst. It's a way we can almost rewrite what actually happened, we try to rewrite the pain and turn it all into triumph.

No one in the universe had more legitimate reasons to take either of these paths than Jesus. Yet, his trials led him to sympathy. He is willing to sympathize with a people whose trials will always be minute compared to his. Are you willing to sympathize with people whose struggles seem really small to you? Are you willing to feel the hardship they're feeling in such a way that it leads them to the throne of grace?

We have some trials with our son, and I pray it is leading us to bigger love and sympathy for any and all trials, big and small. I felt early on when things were unfolding with Titus a need to harden myself to other people's pain. My fear and pain over possibly losing him was so great that I couldn't bear to really feel other people's hardships. This is not God's way. I am learning that grief cannot outdo love. No matter how deep it goes, it cannot consume the love of the Father in Jesus.

Father God: Keep our hearts tender as we go through trials. Help us to remember that the resurrection is real and that all of our hopes are set on it. Thank you for Jesus and His perfect sacrifice on our behalf.

aug 24, 2016
June 30, 2024

Simply Waiting
by Crystal Jolin

Psalm 40:1 (NLT)
I waited patiently for the Lord, He turned to me and heard my cry...

A few years ago, my husband and I had two children and I was newly pregnant with our third. We were sensing a leading from God that we should move back to my hometown. We really loved where we were but knew that it wasn't to be our home long-term. We contacted a couple of people back home to keep their ear out for potential jobs. We heard back almost immediately! A job would be created; they just needed to work out a few things and would be in touch.

Wow - God was providing so simply and on our timetable! How ideal. So we waited for word on the job. And waited. We followed up, got positive feedback, and then waited. And waited. While waiting, spring turned into summer, the days grew hot. And my belly grew. There's nothing like a growing belly to cause a woman's anxiety and need-to-control increase even more quickly than the rising temperatures in July.

All of the details of our possible move swarmed in my head as summer turned into fall: would the job come through, where should we move, when should I tell my employer, would the job work out, would our house sell, etc? And would all of this happen by the time the baby arrived?!

There were so many details that didn't seem to make sense and God was seemingly silent about the details. I was in a season of waiting. And God met me there.

Our pastor began a series on waiting and I knew God was speaking directly to me through the words. I quickly decided to read all the verses in the Bible about waiting. I started at Psalm 40 and that's as far as I got.

David begins that Psalm by stating that he waited patiently. So cliché, but the words still jumped out at me. What wasn't cliché was the profound lesson ahead. I read Psalm 40 and noticed what David did (or was to do) and what God did while David waited.

David was to: wait patiently for the Lord, cry out to Him, and proclaim Him to others.

God: turned to listen, heard him, lifted him out of a pit, set him on solid ground, steadied him as he walked along, gave him a new song, caused others to trust Himself, caused many miracles, had plans for David, and He thought about him.

David's list is so much shorter than God's list! God didn't require much of him. Psalm 40 speaks of God's character, so I knew the same would be true in my relationship with God. It wasn't just for David.

God requires so little of me in any season of waiting. I try so hard to be strong and capable, yet the things that God is doing in my life are so much more complex and imperative. He is working out 10,000 things, while I may see only 3; because He sees all that is in front of me and behind me and around me.

Waiting is either now, or it will come. Whatever that waiting looks like, I can lean in to discover the character of God.

Who *is* He? While I wait, my ability to trust Him hinges on how well I know Him.

Dear Jesus: I wait on You in _____. It is hard to wait! I know you hear my cry. You lift me up. You set me on a rock. You give me a new song in my heart. You love me unfailingly. And so I trust You, knowing You are good. I praise You for all you are doing while I wait. Amen.

Aug. 27, 2016
July 1, 2024

In His Vineyard
by Debbi Ladwig

John 15:1,4,5 (NASB)
"I am the true vine, and my Father is the vinedresser...
Abide in Me, and I in you. As the branch cannot bear fruit of itself,
unless it abides in the vine, so neither can you, unless you abide in Me.
I am the vine, you are the branches..."

Every year, as winter dawdles in making its exit, I get a little impatient waiting for the world to blossom with the new life of springtime. It's a great time to purchase and bring cut flowers into the house.

A bouquet of white carnations makes a beautiful addition to the ambience of a room. However, a more appealing contribution to the environment is a colorful spray – made possible by immersing the cut stems of those same flowers in water dyed in a variety of hues. The stems steadily "drink" the tinted water until – over time – vibrant color permeates the petals. The purples please, the pinks cheer and the yellows delight. Together, they improve the quality of their surroundings.

This year, as a lengthy illness dawdles in making its exit, I have found myself getting a little impatient waiting for newness of life to put some spring back into my step. But these past several months have been a great time for the Lord to teach me some things about life in His vineyard.

I John 5:12 tells us that, *He who has the Son has life.* Jesus, in His teaching about the vineyard in John 15, explains that just as a branch is dependent upon the vine to give it life, we are reliant upon Him – His Words, His love – to infuse us with life.

Botanically speaking, the vine is the life source for many branches. The collective body of Christ can be likened to my bouquet of carnations. As each of us is immersed in the Word and His love, we drink deeply of the living water about which Jesus speaks to the woman of Samaria (see John 4). Vibrancy of life permeates the very being of each branch.

The pray-ers pray – as naturally as they breathe. The encouragers speak or write health-filled, hope-filled words. The wise share truth from the One who is the Truth. Joy and peace are spread; goodness and kindness blossom; faithfulness and gentleness flourish. Love abounds.

I have learned that, together, we improve the quality of our surroundings. And those outside the garden who glimpse His vineyard are sure to be attracted by what they see.

Holy God: Thank you that as I abide in You – as I draw nourishment from Your Word, as I drink deeply of Your love – You abide in me. I pray that I would understand – in its fullness – the privilege of living in Your vineyard. I pray for fruitfulness so that I may enjoy the blessing of both giving and receiving.

God's Sweet Invitation
by Hannah Nobles

Romans 8:28 (The Voice)
We are confident that God is able to orchestrate everything to work toward something good and beautiful when we love Him and accept His invitation to live according to His plan.

I will never forget how my brother Jack sounded when I heard him tell me that our cousin was dead.

"Hannah....He's gone..Jed's gone.."

Our cousin, brother, son, grandchild Jedidiah Wilson, exactly my age, was in a car accident that morning around 8am on his way to the family farm to start another day at work. Our family is close to one another, so when we heard the news, time just....stopped.

When Jack called, I do not remember exactly what happened. All I remember was seeing white and hearing screaming. When my mind caught up with me I realized I was the one screaming. Hot tears drenched my sleeves. The words playing over and over in my head. *Jed's gone. Jed's gone. Jed's gone.*

The ride to Iowa was longer than ever. My parents had been visiting my husband and me in Atlanta, and the news shattered plans and caused a hasty departure for the four of us. No one could talk, no one wanted to make conversation. Fifteen hours in a car, racing back to the family farm to grieve with family was torture.

I answered calls for my mom because she could not speak. I posted updates on social media because words somehow made something crazy more real. And words are therapy. I remember people texting, calling, messaging my family and praying for us. Oh, that sweet, sustaining prayer.

Then, my grandma, also Jed's grandma, texted me. This grandma we all share, who is a spiritual giant even though she is barely 5 feet "short." This is my grandma who loves each of her grandchildren so well and wore out her jeans kneeling before God and praying fervently for all of us before we even had names.

She texted: "God's best isn't always our best …we have just opened the door into the room He has chosen. We will walk with Him into this unfamiliar place as He provides the furnishings."

Man, what powerful words at the beginning of what will be a tough season!

This world is kind of like a giant house that God walks us through. Sometimes we settle in a room that is comfortable to us. It has our comfy bed with fluffy pillows. Our precious toys that we love to play with. However, sometimes God takes our hand and asks us to go with Him to another room. When we walk in, it is discordant with our familiar room. The new space does not have our favorite toys, nor our comfy bed with fluffy pillows. We can choose to get angry, be upset with Him, pout and ask, "Why?! Why are You bringing us to THIS room?!" We can even say, "I want to go back to the other room!"

Or, we can choose to surrender our comfort. We can choose to take hold of our Creator God's hand, the One that knows our heart so well, and trust that He has a plan for us and that room. A plan to display His love so that the world may know who He is. May we accept His invitation to embark with Him into unfamiliar territory, and may we trust Him in every season of the soul.

Lord, in the midst of a new season, help me embrace your invitation to follow you into the unknown. Help my heart to trust in your guidance. Thank you for leading me well!

Aug 28, 2016
July 7, 2024

Even When...
by Michelle Pearson

Matthew 28:30 (NASB)
"...and lo, I am with you always, even to the end of the age."

It's THAT call. The one that, if thought about ahead of time, makes our knees drop from beneath us, our heart race, and our brow drip with sweat.

Mine came about 8:45 on June 16, 2014. My Dad. A fall. Not going to make it. My mom sounded so calm as she told me to come immediately.

And lo, I am with you always ...even when the bad news comes.

After a few minutes of intense wailing and rushed packing, I found myself speeding north – of course through driving rain and powerful lightening coupled with tornado warnings the entire time. For those three + hours I spent most of the time questioning, "Are you sure, Lord? Are you sure this can be your plan? What about all the years I thought he had left? Are you sure?"

And lo, I am with you always ...even when you doubt.

As anyone who has experienced a sudden death understands, life operates on autopilot for a while. Endless meetings – funeral home director, florist, caterer. Endless greetings – local townspeople with fabulous food, faithful friends from all eras, extended family who come from afar. Endless fear – Did he suffer? How will we survive? Who will take care of my mom?

And lo, I am with you always ...even when you are not sure what to do next.

Jesus' final words. His last chance to impress wisdom on his disciples, and he reminds them that he is there. Wherever. Whenever.

In the weeks following my dad's death, I purposed to identify wherever I saw God working. Wherever I knew His profound presence carried me. There were plenty of well intentioned comments reminding me of how tragic this time was. More inspiring, more motivating would be to be mindful of how often He surrounded me with His sovereign touch and unfailing love.

- learning that Dad suffered a severe heart attack and died as quickly as he always hoped he would… *"and lo, I am with you always…"*
- experiencing sweet unity with my sisters and mom as we endured an emotionally and physically draining week… *"and lo, I am with you always…"*
- savoring an uncharacteristically blank personal family calendar in the month that followed… *"and lo, I am with you always…"*

And still now, almost two years later…Where is God?

- He's in the girlfriends that dine with my mom weekly to maintain accountability.
- He's in the mechanic who treats my mom's car like his own.
- He's in the memories we have of my dad calling us while on a walk or driving the boat.
- He's in the passion I have to share the gospel.

Even when I think about my dad and end up in a sulking state of sadness, or a fretful wave of fear, or grateful posture of praise, God is *wherever* I am.

What about you? Do you wallow in your suffering, questioning why God would allow it? Or do you acknowledge His presence in each piece of your heartache?

Dear Lord, Help me to trust your promises – to believe that you are with me wherever I am. Whatever is happening. However I feel. Even when…

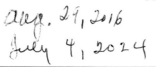

Disappointment Is Never Neutral
by Joseph Romeo

James 3:16 (ESV)
For where jealousy and selfish ambition exist,
there will be disorder and every vile practice.

I wrestled my freshman and sophomore years in high school. I wish I could say things went well, but words fail to adequately describe the fullness of that disaster. I was awful. On one especially humiliating evening, I was the only person on the team who lost. I walked out of the gym, sat down by myself and cried. No matter how hard I practiced, no matter how hard I tried, I had little to show for it. In a word, I was disappointed.

Disappointment isn't necessarily a sin, but it can be. When we fail to get something we want, or when things in our lives don't work out as we had hoped, we get disappointed. At those moments it's appropriate to pause and ask ourselves, "Why am I disappointed?" Sad to say, in my own life (and certainly during my two gloriously sub-par wrestling years) my disappointment often has its roots in selfishness. I get disappointed if I don't get the approval of someone, or I get disappointed if someone's not impressed with something I've said or written.

These are sinful reasons to be disappointed because they stem from "selfish ambition," which, as James tells us is *"not the wisdom that comes down from above, but is earthly, unspiritual, demonic. For where jealousy and selfish ambition exist, there will be disorder and every vile practice"* (James 3:15-16). My disappointment is rooted in unbelief. I fail to believe that God is for me and not against me. I believe he's withholding good from me even though his Word says, *"no good thing does he withhold from those who walk uprightly"* (Ps. 84:11).

I often tell my congregation that one of our most common sins as fallen creatures is trying to satisfy eternal longings with temporal pleasures. One of those "temporal pleasures" is the praise of man. Oh, to what lengths we go to hear others sing our praises! Oh, to what lengths we go to make others think we're something special! Surely Solomon was right: *"The crucible is for silver, and the furnace is for gold, and a man is tested by his praise"* (Prov. 27:21).

Such longing for human praise is folly. Medieval writer Bernard of Clairvaux said, "It is folly and extreme madness always to be longing for things that not only can never satisfy but even blunt the appetite; however much you have of such things, you still desire what you have not yet attained; you are always restlessly sighing after what is missing."[1] Follow your disappointment to the root cause and fight to believe the promises of God.

Prayer: Heavenly Father, our hearts are restless until they rest in you.[2] In your grace, would you show us that idols always lead to disappointment because they can only raise the bar or lower the boom. As I stumble and fall throughout this life, lift my eyes to behold the wonder and glory of your Son, Jesus Christ, and remind me that I stand complete in him. Amen.

---

[1] Bernard of Clairvaux, "On Loving God," in *Bernard of Clairvaux: Selected Works*, ed. Emilie Griffin, tr., G. R. Evans (San Francisco: HarperCollins, 1987), 69.

[2] Augustine, *The Confessions of St. Augustine*, trans. John K. Ryan (NY: Doubleday, 1960), 1.1.

Choices
by Jeannine Sawall

Deuteronomy 30:19 (NIV)
Today I have given you the choice between life and death, between blessings and curses. Now I call on heaven and earth to witness the choice you make. Oh, that you would choose life, so that you and your descendants might live!

I read a blog post by Matt Hammitt that really made me stop and think. He said that tension is the place where the worst of life and the best of true hope meet to unveil our eyes to God's work of redemption. He later says that we are allowed to know great pain, so that we can know the greater pleasure of trading that pain in for purpose.

Matt made this statement regarding his infant son, Bowen. Their family was in the midst of a journey as Bowen was born with a serious heart defect, one that was potentially life threatening. Pictures were posted and my heart ached as I looked at that tiny baby with tubes coming out of everywhere.

Why?? Why such suffering for such a little guy? Why such sorrow and uncertainty for his family? Why such trauma in everyday life for any of us? For me...why 10 miscarriages? Those tiny beings who I loved the moment I knew they existed, lost to us time and time again. Why my mom? The journey of grief continues with her loss. There are moments and days where I'm still overcome with the missing of her. Friends who watch their loved ones waste away with disease? It's easy to go to that place of "why?"

Sin. The Curse. The Fall. The answer to my "whys." Sickness, sorrow, pain, suffering...these are the results of sin, not of God's oversight. God does not bring these difficult times to us.

Sin touches all of our lives. However, God uses these times to draw us to Him, if we let Him. In the midst of living in a world where we can expect suffering, we are given two choices.

We can say He is not enough and turn away, or we can be touched by our gracious and caring God who meets us in the midst of that tension.

We can lean into a God, who in that worst place, will show us there is still purpose. He will reveal to us the character of His being and tell us He has made a way; to hang on, Hope is around the corner. He has redeemed us and a day is coming when all tears will be gone forever.

When we know the secret of His redemptive grace, we can choose to stand in the midst of any trial and say, "He is good!" He is good! He is good! He gives us that choice. We only have to make it for Him.

How will you make the choice to trust God in your suffering?

Lord, help me to trust you during times of suffering and fully know, that despite my circumstances, You are good. Amen.

Aug 30, 2016

July 6, 2024

---

30 - *Suffering*

Questions to Consider/Discuss

1. When you read the hymn that opened this section, what reaction(s) did you have to it?

2. When you read the hymn's author's background, what thoughts did you have about that person's life, circumstances, or character?

3. What entries from this section were the most helpful to you?

4. What Scripture(s) did you find surprising to see in this section?

5. How were you encouraged in this section of the book?

6. What challenges or encouragements would you like to incorporate into your life after reading this section?

7. What is one change you intend to make based on the readings in this section?

32 - *Suffering*

Awake, my soul, and with the sun
Thy daily stage of duty run;
Shake off dull sloth, and joyful rise,
To pay thy morning sacrifice.

Lord, I my vows to Thee renew;
Disperse my sins as morning dew.
Guard my first springs of thought and will,
And with Thyself my spirit fill.

Direct, control, suggest, this day,
All I design, or do, or say,
That all my powers, with all their might,
In Thy sole glory may unite.

Praise God from Whom all blessings flow,
Praise Him all creatures here below,
Praise Him above, ye Heavenly Host.
Praise Father, Son, and Holy Ghost.[2]
Thomas Ken

Hymn Reflection: Community
by Jen Woyke

When I was little we still had Sunday evening service at church. Often those services would end with the congregation singing the *Doxology* a cappella. As a young child I loved the sense of "tradition" that I felt when we sang. Even now, singing the *Doxology* evokes those early memories of being part of a community.

Community seems to be such a "buzz word" these days. But it's nothing new. God himself, from the very moment of creation, has desired for us to be in community with Him. And he desires us to be in community with one another too. You only have to read a few verses of Genesis to know that God has made us for community.

Thomas Ken wrote what we commonly call the *Doxology* as part of a set of hymns while he was school master in the late 1600's. They were written to help guide the devotional time of his young pupils. The boys at the school were encouraged to sing the songs daily. There was a song for the morning, the evening and midnight (if they were unable to sleep or were awakened). Each verse ended with the doxology portion *Praise God from whom all blessings flow...* Whether it was sung individually, or with a group, the boys knew others were raising the same words in praise to God.

As the boys lived in community, they practiced community by singing truth together and separately. *Praise God from whom all blessings flow...* God is the giver of every good thing. We owe Him our very lives. *Praise Him all creatures here below...* Everything we do, the very way we live, should bring praise to Him. *Praise Him above ye heavenly hosts. Praise Father, Son and Holy Ghost.* God, the originator of community, desires to be in community with you. Wherever you are, in the midst of a God-honoring community of believers, or alone with your Savior, let that amazing thought buoy you today! *Amen.*

God of my Couch
AND God of "Out There"
by Courtney Aronson

✺ Ecclesiastes 4:9-10 (NIV)
Two are better than one, because they have a good return for their labor: If either of them falls down, one can help the other up. But pity anyone who falls and has no one to help them up.

I have this giant, fluffy couch here in my college house. There is nothing really special about it, minus the fact that it's right outside my room, making it the prime location to be when I come home from class. This couch is good. Sometimes, okay who am I kidding, a lot of my time this school year has been spent on this couch.

Now, one of the sweetest things in all of life is spending time with Jesus alone. I love it. I can't get enough of Him. But for some reason that I don't even know how to put into words, I felt that the only place I would truly experience God was there, on my couch, specifically in the morning (naturally with a vanilla latte in my hands), digging into His Word. Does God show up in those times? ABSOLUTELY! But sometimes, when I try to live the life of faith on my own, I start believing that God only shows up in certain and marked out ways (hence the couch; not to mention, it's kind of an ugly brown). That sounds pretty limiting and like I don't expect to see Him *wherever.*

Well, I've got to say, if it were not for my community, I would not have realized how silly I was being. Expecting God to show up only in the parts of the day that were specifically penciled in as my "time with God".

37 - Community

Friends, if we truly believe that God is *wherever*, that means expecting Him to show up, lavish His love on us, convict us, lead us, not only in the times that we invite Him in, but throughout the live-long day!

One of my dear friends that I have had since ninth grade goes to college with me. She can probably give you more details about my life than I could ever come up with. Not long ago, I was--wait for it, can you guess where I was?--that's right, on that couch, and my sweet friend asked me how I was doing. I thought I was doing fine, but when I began to speak, tears started streaming like the Jordan. Let me tell ya! I poured out to her my frustrations about not connecting with God in my time that I had dedicated to Him.

My dear friend spoke a few gentle yet resounding words, "Courtney, of course God wants to show up in your time spent with Him. But God is not limited to showing up only on this couch. Of course, He wants to show you more of His character when you read His Word, but He is out there too!" As she said this, she pointed out into the world.

It was silly that I couldn't figure that out on my own. But God puts community around us to grab our chins and turn our heads to look at the face of Jesus. Friends, God is in your quiet times, but He wants to show you that He is truly *wherever*.

Beautiful Lord, please open up my eyes to see you throughout the day through your Spirit. And show me that you are limitless!

Called to Encourage
by Elizabeth Bender

Hebrews 10:24-25 (ESV)
And let us consider how to stir up one another to love and good works, not neglecting to meet together, as is the habit of some, but encouraging one another, and all the more as you see the Day drawing near.

Five months. It has been five months since I have felt *normal*. Within the last month I finally found an answer to why I continue to never feel quite 100%. I was diagnosed with strep induced reactive arthritis. To make a long story short, my body kept producing strep antibodies even after the bacteria was gone and those antibodies began to attack my joints which causes swelling and pain. The hope is that I can now begin treatment to counter the actual problem and though it may take awhile my body will eventually go back to *normal*.

I am currently a student at Baylor University in Waco, TX which is a little over 1,200 miles away from my home in Bismarck, ND. I love going to school here and love the people that I have encountered on and off campus. Living far away from home, however, does not work well with being sick for such a long time. There are days when all I want is my mommy and my daddy. Many days I feel alone in this struggle. What I have come to realize over the past five months though, is that I am not alone in this struggle.

Over the course of the past month, this has really hit home with me in two specific ways. The first realization that I am not alone came through a friend at church repeatedly telling me she could set up a meal train for me. Other individuals at the church I attend here in Waco, Calvary Baptist Church, would bring me food two times a week for a few weeks. She asked many times and each time I declined. Eventually, I said yes. I came to the realization that this is what the body of Christ does for one another. By being in community with fellow believers we enter into an unspoken contract to meet the needs of those with whom we fellowship. In the past, I have fulfilled this role for others. But now I have to give up control of my situation, realize that I need help, appreciate that there are others who are willing to help, and be humbled that I am surrounded by the body of Christ when I am in need. I will say this is not easy. Admitting that I need help and then asking for help does not come easy. I had to realize that sometimes I am on the receiving end of Christian hospitality.

The second realization came to me on a recent Sunday morning. It was a tough morning where I did not want to get out of bed. I had to remind myself how much I love going to church. I got up and went to Calvary. I am so glad I did. Many came up to me asking how I was doing and telling me that they were praying for me. I received great encouragement that morning not only from the service but also from my Christ family. This was a great reminder to me that I am loved, but also of the great importance of meeting with our church families.

My hope is that you are inspired to make time for community, spending meaningful time with one another, but that you are also inspired to learn from, to receive from, and to give to one another.

Heavenly Father, may I continue meeting with my Christian community and realize the importance of this time. And help me to remember that being a part of a Christian community means that I am called to give, but that I am also called to receive. Release me from my pride so I am humbled as I receive from my community. Amen!

Sept. 2, 2016

April 6, 2017

July 8, 2020

Unity in Our Differences
by Stacy Bender

1 Peter 3:38 (NLT)
Finally, all of you should be of one mind. Sympathize with each other. Love each other as brothers and sisters. Be tenderhearted and keep a humble attitude.

I grew up attending Mendenhall Presbyterian Church in East Grand Forks, MN, on Sundays. Because my dad had grown up Catholic, our family would often attend midnight mass on Christmas Eve. I found the services beautiful and mysterious there. Oddly, my husband – a Baptist minister – now serves as a chaplain at a Catholic university.

I did not internalize what the word *liturgy* was as a child. In fact, it was not until I started to attend Grace Baptist Church as a teen that I realized that some churches had a very similar liturgy (Lutherans, Methodists, Presbyterians) while others had their own vein of liturgy.

Those with their own veins of liturgy often attempt to claim they are without liturgy; however, once I realized what liturgy was, it became clear that all churches have it whether they realize it or not.

Liturgy essentially means the rhythm with which we do church. Some people would call it a service schedule, but it is more than that.

Each part of the service has a theological significance, and the liturgy of a church can reveal its theology. Even the location of the podium in relation to the altar/communion table reveals part of the specific church's liturgy.

For example, in the Baptist tradition, the Word of God and its interpretation (the sermon) are central to the service. The podium from which the pastor preaches the sermon would typically be in the center of the stage.

In contrast, for a Catholic tradition, the Eucharist (communion) is central which is why the podium remains off to the side with the altar in the center.

As Ash Wednesday approached this year, I felt a pull toward the liturgical side of this day. Had I grown up in the churches I have attended in later years, I might not even know what Ash Wednesday was. I chose to attend a Methodist church this year.

As the pastor described that he had prepared the ashes for last evening by burning the palm branches used in last year's Palm Sunday service, I was moved. As another pastor read Psalm 51 aloud, I was moved. As the small group who had gathered to worship together sang songs that directed our minds to the saving work that Christ did on the cross, I was moved.

Being moved did not come from anything that they did but rather what I did in obedience to **worship, to remember, and to consider.**

As I drove away from the church service, I marveled at the unity we have with others who believe in the uniqueness of Christ. Because of that unity, I could walk into almost any Christian church in almost any town in almost any country around the world and worship next to people with whom I likely have differences.

The world will know God's love through Christ when we come together and worship in love.

Father God, help us to love others who believe in you but with whom we may disagree. Help us to be tenderhearted and humble in our interactions. Give us grace when we lack the desire to do this because of our own pride.

Church Community Hurts
by Jason Esposito

1 Corinthians 1:10-11 (NIV)

I appeal to you, brothers, in the name of our Lord Jesus Christ,
that all of you agree with one another
so that there may be no divisions among you
and that you may be perfectly united in mind and thought.
My brothers, some from Chloe's household have informed
me that there are quarrels among you.

I continually stay committed to running and working out. I know that it is good for me physically and psychologically. It gives me energy and builds endurance, but it just hurts and reminds me I am not a 17 year old cross-country runner anymore. If I am to stay in optimal running shape, there will be a certain level of pain.

Any time you gather a group of people together, you are going to have a high potential for pain. All of us have very different backgrounds, personalities, preferences, genetic wiring, and spiritual understanding. We are male and female. We are young and old. All this creates great opportunity, but also great pain.

Church hurts because conflict is always part of community on this side of eternity; when you get a bunch of different people together, there will be pain.

Do you sit back and dream about the "Good Old Days" when gas was only $1.00 a gallon? We tend to have a skewed picture of the past. If we could only go back to how church used to be, we would have no pain, no struggles, and no conflict.

The good old days of the church in biblical times must have been some utopian experience.

---

43 - Community

Was it? No, what we discover is that Paul wrote a vast portion of the New Testament letters to the church to help them resolve the pain, the conflict of church.

The conflict in the early church ranged from personality conflicts, preferences over which preacher people liked, theological and financial issues, to honesty, and issues over membership, to name a few. The fact that church hurts has always been, and always will be, true because church is a community, and authentic community is crazy hard.

The bottom line is that if you stay at any church for a given amount of time, you will experience pain. The pastor will disappoint you. Church leaders will disappoint you. You won't agree with every decision that is made. A program that you love and think is core to the church will end. The music will change. The church will get bigger or smaller. A close friend will leave the church. Someone will offend you. A friendship will be broken. You won't get the call back. All your expectations won't be met. This kind of thing will happen because we are broken people on the pilgrimage called Christianity existing in this community called church, and we are constantly leaking out the truth of who we must be as Christians.

Church will always have some level of emotional and relational pain. Yet, Jesus compels us to be unified even in the middle of the pain of church.

In John, Jesus prayed for us, "My prayer is not for them alone. I pray also for those who will believe in me through their message!"

Never forget that Jesus prayed for you. That is amazing. Jesus knew we would get upset in church community; he knew we would be discouraged and so he prayed for us. He prayed that we would see the pain through and be unified. Is there a greater encouragement?!

Dear Heavenly Father help me to be an advocate for unity in the church. Help me to see that the difficulty of community can be the environment of greatest growth as a follower of Jesus Christ.

Lonely in a Crowd
by Dina Hanken

Hebrews 13:14 (NIV)
For here we do not have an enduring city,
but we are looking for the city that is to come.

I have been a follower of Jesus for most of my life. My earliest memories are of preschool Sunday School. I clearly remember Miss Betty and her colorful Bible story pictures. Every week I attended church. It was the hub of my family's spiritual teaching as well as our social life. Our best friends were at church.

In post-modern church speak, we had found our "community." In my forty plus years, I have had the privilege of experiencing Christian community through every stage of my life. I have known the joy of belonging. Christian community is not perfect...not even close...but God's body design was not a mistake, and life within a Christian community is the Creator's desire for our lives.

So what if you are lonely? You are involved with a group of believers, and still you find yourself feeling alone even among those you love and call family. I have been experiencing a bit of this in my life recently, and it has caused me to think more about loneliness.

If you find yourself in this un-enviable position, can I share a few thoughts with you?

Maybe you are lonely because you are not from here. Hebrews 13:14 clearly states that as believers, we are not from here. 1 Peter 2:11 goes so far as to call us "*aliens*" in this world. When God created Adam and Eve, He created them to live in a perfect world. Not to be overly critical...but have you looked around lately? THIS is not perfect. Could your lonely feelings be caused by homesickness?

Maybe you are lonely because you have found your best friend…and He is not from here. When I made the choice to follow Jesus, I literally made a new best friend. Immediately I received the Holy Spirit and have the amazing gift of God's presence in me at all times. I talk with Jesus constantly and I know He hears me. I read His word and learn to know Him more. But do you ever just want to see Him…to have Him hold you and smile into your face? Me too. Maybe you are lonely because your best friend, the perfect lover of your soul, lives in heaven.

Maybe you are lonely because you believe the promise. Before Jesus left Earth, He told his disciples, "*I am going there to prepare a place for you…*" (John 14:2) This world is NOT all there is. I remind myself of this when a situation seems particularly hopeless.

Hebrews 11 recounts the lives of many faithful Jesus followers and a very telling phrase in verse 16 that they were "*longing for a better country- a heavenly one.*" That sounds a little lonely to me.

Even though we may "long for a better country" along with the believers listed in Hebrews, we do have something that they did not…the body of Christ!

Let's not forget to take every advantage of opportunities to encourage and be encouraged by other Jesus followers. It may not be heaven…but it can feel pretty close sometimes!

Lord, sometimes even in a crowd we can feel lonely. Thank you for being such a good God that has given us SO much to look forward to! Help us to be faithfully involved with a body of believers who are also longing for their heavenly home. Very good !

Sept 5, 2016
April 13, 2017
Oct. 30, 2017
July 11, 2024

Whoever Loves God
MUST Also Love His Brother
by Pastor John McNabb

1 John 2:9, 4:21 (NIV)
Anyone who claims to be in the light but hates his brother is still in the darkness. And He has given us this command: Whoever loves God must also love his brother.

I disliked him intensely! My parents taught us not to say the word hate, but in reality, I hated him. He was rude, self-absorbed, and a know it all. My hatred for him festered like a splinter in my finger. Each day it got more infected. I wasn't sleeping well, I wasn't eating, my attitude towards others was strained and I felt far from God.

A friend noticed that I had not been myself. My attitude was not as joyful as it normally was. He asked me if there was a problem. I talked with him about my feelings and he prayed with me. We walked together through that difficult time. He shared this verse in 1 John about loving our brothers and then we looked through a book entitled, *Victory Over the Darkness* by Neil Anderson. I used the Bible and book to work through my issue.

I came to realize that my entire person; physical, emotional, and spiritual health were being affected by my hatred. I confessed my sin and worked with God on repentance. In a short time I felt released from my sin, forgiven and in right relationship with God. My relationship with the person improved too. God was working on my heart!

There was a time where I would have said that I can't love that person. Maybe you feel that way toward a person in your life. Maybe they have said something hurtful or done something to you to cause you great pain. Scripture teaches us from 1 John 4:21 that if I love God I "MUST" love my brother. When I began to show love toward my brother, in time, I was able to think about him without feeling hurt, anger or resentment. It was awesome!

The Bible says in 1 Peter 5:8, "*Your enemy the devil prowls around like a roaring lion looking for someone to devour.*" The devil knows that if he can plant the seed of hatred in your heart he can devour your Christian testimony. So 1 Peter 5:8 begins with these words, "*Be clear- minded and alert...*" If you feel hatred growing in your heart, capture that feeling and give it to Jesus.

I just finished preaching a 30 week sermon series from the Bible. Can you guess what Bible book it was from? If you guessed 1 John you would be right. It's my favorite Bible book. Check it out!

Lord, please look into my heart and see if I may be harboring hatred. If I am please show me and give me the strength and wisdom to love others as you have loved me.

Sept. 12, 2016
April 13, 2017
Oct. 30, 2017
July 11, 2024

New Family
by Shan Reed

Mark 10:29-30 (NIV)

"Truly I tell you," Jesus replied, "no one who has left home or brothers or sisters or mother or father or children or fields for Me and the gospel will fail to receive a hundred times as much in this present age: homes, brothers, sisters, mothers, children and fields – along with persecutions – and in the age to come eternal life."

I grew up in a small town in South Dakota. Pretty much all of my classmates had extended family that lived nearby, or at least within a couple of hours. My *closest* relatives lived in Kansas, a nine-hour drive from our home.

The benefit of having relatives who lived all over the United States was that we got to visit many places and take in sights around the country.

The bummer was that my grandparents, aunts, uncles, and cousins did not get to attend my band concerts and church Christmas programs, and vice versa. Holidays were almost always spent with just the four of us in my immediate family.

I was jealous of those other kids who had relatives around all the time. I wanted my grandma to teach me how to sew or my grandpa to teach my how to drive a nail into a board.

As time went by, our community, especially our church community, started to include my family in their families' celebrations. My friends' grandparents became my other grandparents. My friends' parents became my second parents.

I learned to sew, not only from my mom but also from my friend's mom. I learned to chop weeds in the bean fields from my friend's dad. I learned to shoot a jump shot, not only from my own dad but also from my dad's friend. I called my friends' grandma "Gram" just like they did. I called my church friends' grandma "Grandma Honey" just like they did.

We celebrated Thanksgiving with Grandma Honey's family. We celebrated Christmas and New Year's with other families from church. We spent summer vacation traveling around the U.S. visiting our relatives.

My parents and our church community taught me what Jesus told His disciples, *"No one who has left home... for Me... will fail to receive a hundred times..."* (Mark 10:29-30NIV).

Wherever you go, you will have family.

Now I live in Japan, even farther from family and friends. I left a job and a church family I loved because Jesus said, "Come, follow Me." Yet, even though the distance between me and all I once knew as comfortable and familiar has grown farther, Jesus has given me a new community.

I see how He has given me a hundred times what I left behind. Now I have more moms and dads and brothers and sisters, aunts and uncles, nephews and nieces. And, this can happen even in another language all because of Jesus' love.

I have a new community, a larger community. My parents, the church and the community in which I was raised, all taught me the joys of becoming family with those who are not biologically related.

Are there people in your community who don't have a grandma nearby or who spend holidays alone or who just seem lonely? Invite them over to your house; invite them to your band concert; take a moment to say hello. You never know the new family member you may find when you open your heart.

Dear Jesus, may those who feel far from family and friends and comfort, today, be encouraged by Your promises. May each of us reach out to those around us and include them in our family just as You have included us in Your family.

Sept 7, 2016
July 12, 2024

Made for Each Other
by Shane Rothlisberger

Genesis 2:18 (HCSB)
Then the LORD God said, "It is not good for the man to be alone."

Over a decade ago my wife and I moved to Northeast Iowa to serve on staff with a small church in a rural community. While we loved the area and were excited about the mission before us, we very quickly found ourselves missing the abundance of relationships we had formed at our previous church. And unfortunately, a quick survey of the demographic landscape revealed there wasn't exactly a surplus of young families around.

So we took a risk. We approached the two other couples we knew, and convinced them to start a weekly small group with us in our home. The idea would be to eat, talk, study God's Word, and pray together. It was a simple recipe, and thankfully, God blessed it. We were craving community, and it quickly became apparent we weren't the only ones. Within a year's time the six of us morphed into 36. The living room of our little home was at max capacity, and we were forced to make the difficult, yet appropriate decision to multiply our group. One became three, and God used those small groups to breathe new life into our little church, as many put their trust in Jesus, responded in baptism, and became integral members of God's household.

"It is not good for man to be alone."

God's Word begins and ends with weddings. The former takes place in a garden between the first man and woman. The latter occurs in a city between a people and their God. And throughout the pages between these two grand covenantal ceremonies, this truth resounds: *we were made for community.*

God's proclamation in the garden of the malevolence of loneliness reveals that He has rooted within His people an innate need for one another. It is but a taste of what is true of God Himself. For within the mystery of the Trinity, perfect community has existed from eternity past. God the Father, God the Son, and God the Holy Spirit, communing and delighting in one another in perfect unity.

As those fashioned in His image, we are privileged to experience but a sampling of this attribute of God. Furthermore, God's design for community reaches beyond our joy and becomes paramount to the advancement of the gospel. An unbelieving world ought to look into the community of God's people and observe something supremely attractive: People loving, serving, blessing, and enjoying one another.

In contrast, the enemy despises Biblical community. He hates the "one anothers," and one of his greatest strategies is to lead God's people into isolation. His subtle lies perpetuate the notion that there is power and freedom in independence. In reality, liberation is found in dependence. Dependence upon God and each other.

Christian, embrace community. Orient your life around the people of God in your local church, partnering together to be an irresistible influence in a world that is longing to belong.

Prayer: Father, thank You for the gospel that not only redeems and reconciles us to You as well as to each other. Thank You for giving us a community of believers to carry out the mission you have called us to. Grant us faithfulness in our love for You and our love for Your people. Amen.

Aug 8, 2016
Sept. 21, 2017
July 15, 2024

Blue Chicago
by Shelley Schmor

Zephaniah 3:17 (NLT)

For the Lord your God is living among you. He is a mighty savior. He will take delight in you with gladness. With his love, he will calm all your fears. He will rejoice over you with joyful songs.

It was one of those weeks when your soul feels beat up and wounded and you know the only thing that could tangibly help is a change of venue, a time away. So, off to Chicago, was where I found myself accompanied by my man, my favorite human. As we arrived, frigid temperatures and whipping winds tried to deter us. But, we dug in our heels determined to experience a weekend of rest and renewal. We checked into our hotel, the valet parked our car and we made our way to our room where we were greeted by an amazing view of Lake Michigan.

We soon realized we had no plan, no agenda, just two days ahead of us, and we were hungry. Grabbing our coats, we headed to the closest McDonald's for a snack. We walked into a room filled with mostly homeless people and an atmosphere of sadness and desperation which permeated your soul. I would love to tell you that my first inclination was to "love on" all these people and "minister to their hurting souls". But it wasn't. I was too enraptured in my own pain to even think about someone else's. I know, I know, how selfish....right?

Or is it? Selfish, that is? Or maybe, do we need to come to a place of receiving healing so that we can speak healing to others?

Our snack consumed, we made our way back to our room for a highly anticipated nap. An hour later, awakening a bit tired and foggy, we renewed our determination to experience our urban healing. We headed to the beautiful lobby where the desk clerk gave us suggestions for dinner and entertainment. After a few minutes of deliberation we agreed on a restaurant and set out to fill our stomachs.

Mission accomplished. With our appetites filled, we were ready for some entertainment and were excited to take in some Chicago Blues. Just across the street *Blue Chicago*, with its neon sign, beckoned us. As my eyes adjusted to the dark and close quarters we found ourselves in, I soon felt as though we were being welcomed into a family reunion of sorts. The music began and *Mike Wheeler* and his band transported us to that place that only blues music can take you. Music that is filled with tones and sounds that are steeped in old spiritual undertones. Music you sing when you are sad.

And there, at *Blue Chicago*, a deep healing began to take place. The music connected to my soul in ways that only the Spirit could. My culmination of healing occurred when *Demetria Taylor* took the stage and urged the women in the club to make their way to the dance floor. It was there that she declared on us a call to liberation and freedom. A call to love one another, to love ourselves. A reminder that we are all part of this same human family. We don't need to compare ourselves to each other. We don't need to beat each other up and tear each other down. Instead we can love and be loved together in community. So, there, in *Blue Chicago*, a club filled with people of every kind - male, female, black, white, Latino, Asian, gay, straight - Jesus met me and His Spirit deeply healed me. Does Jesus meet me - wherever? YES! Even at a nlues club in the heart of Chicago! Now, let's get to that healing of others......

Father, give me ears to hear your voice singing over me today. Help me notice it wherever it may come from - even through the voice of a Blues singer in Chicago. Bring healing to my soul and life to my dry bones - so that in my healing, I can heal others.

Surrounded
by Austin Walker

Genesis 12: 1 & 4 (NIV)

The Lord had said to Abram, "Go from your country,
your people and your father's household to the land I will show you."
So Abram went, as the Lord had told him; and Lot went with him.
Abram was seventy-five years old when he set out from Harran.

It was mid-October, and I was helping my brother with a construction project. I found myself standing on the top of a building in northern Minnesota when my cell phone rang. On the other end of the phone was someone I had grown to respect from a distance (that sounds creepy – stick with me).

After the general "Hey, how are you" of the conversation, he said, "I want to ask you if you would be willing to come and work with me? I have a position open, and I think you would be great for it!"

My wife and I had just had our third child three weeks earlier. This was not an opportunity I was expecting and, as the job was out-of-state, I frankly wasn't even interested. I had a job I liked, my family was growing, and my boys had just started a new school.

God had continued to bless the work I was doing, and we had a group of people who had become more like family than friends over the past 8 years. Accepting this position would require moving my family to a new state, finding a new school for my boys, and being away from the community we had grown to love and need.

To make everything even crazier, the job started January first - just ten weeks away. My questions were growing, along with my feelings of uncertainty and fear. I wanted to follow God's calling on my life.

Through conversations with my family, friends and mentors, my wife and I felt that God was calling us to trust Him. He was calling us to go, even though we didn't know what the future held. Through this process, God revealed to me how important it is to be surrounded by people who love you, love Jesus, and push you to follow Him no matter the cost.

The story of Abram's calling was a place where I found great comfort while wrestling with the possibility of this new endeavor. In verse 1 it says, *"Go from your country, your people and your father's household to the land I will show you."* God called Abram to leave his people, his family, and follow God's calling.

Like Abram, I had no idea what we were stepping into or where God was taking us. But those in our closest circle had confirmed what we were feeling, so we knew that God was calling us away from our current life, our family and our comfort. It was incredibly difficult to leave, but looking back, God has blessed us more than we ever could have imagined. Our relationships with our community have grown deeper and wider in a way I never could have dreamed it would.

What does the community of people you have around you look like? Is it a group of people that encourage you to follow Jesus? What are some areas that God may be calling you to trust Him and step out in faith?

God, thank You for those You have surrounded me with that love me and love You. I trust You. What do You want from me? I am willing to follow You wherever You lead me. Thank You for loving me, calling me, claiming me, and saving me!

Sept. 13, 2016
Sept 20, 2017
July 17, 2024

Questions to Consider/Discuss

1. When you read the hymn that opened this section, what reaction(s) did you have to it?

2. When you read the hymn's author's background, what thoughts did you have about that person's life, circumstances, or character?

3. What entries from this section were the most helpful to you? *allow others to help you*

4. What Scripture(s) did you find surprising to see in this section?

5. How were you encouraged in this section of the book?

6. What challenges or encouragements would you like to incorporate into your life after reading this section?

7. What is one change you intend to make based on the readings in this section? *Forgiveness* *& forgive*

"Pain" of church - early Church had problems. With Gods help we can solve them. Codef does such a good job in this area.

Be willing to accept help.

Forgive my brother/sister.

57 - *Community*

Come, thou Fount of every blessing,
tune my heart to sing thy grace;
streams of mercy, never ceasing,
call for songs of loudest praise.
Teach me some melodious sonnet,
sung by flaming tongues above.
Praise the mount!
I'm fixed upon it,
mount of thy redeeming love.

Here I raise mine Ebenezer;
hither by thy help I'm come;
and I hope, by thy good pleasure,
safely to arrive at home.
Jesus sought me when a stranger,
wandering from the fold of God;
He, to rescue me from danger,
interposed his precious blood.

O to grace how great a debtor
daily I'm constrained to be!
Let thy goodness,
like a fetter, bind my wandering heart to thee.
Prone to wander,
Lord, I feel it,
prone to leave the God I love;
here's my heart,
O take and seal it,
seal it for thy courts above.[3]
Robert Robinson

---

60 - Wandering

Hymn Reflection: Wandering
by Jen Woyke

Bind my wandering heart to thee...

Robert Robinson, who wrote *Come, Thou Fount of Every Blessing*, came to Christ in a fairly dramatic way after living a life of petty theft, vandalism, and carousing. The story goes that much later in his life he found himself wandering from God again and was challenged by a lady quoting the very words he had written.

The first time I read his story it nearly made me cry. It was so sad, yet as I think about it, I know that, all too often, it is my story too. And maybe yours. My wandering doesn't often take the form of doubt. I don't doubt God's goodness even in the midst of difficult circumstances—in fact those are often the times I feel the closest to God—the times I most realize my reliance on Him. More often, my wandering comes through living everyday life. I get too busy, I get too focused on a project or a job or a person and I forget that my first love should be God. *Prone to wander, Lord I feel it, prone to leave the God I love...*

Bind my wandering heart to thee is a prayer I need to utter again and again. It's a reminder that we are by nature wandering creatures who need to be constantly reminded of the God who loved us so much He gave His Son for our lives.

As you read, or sing, these words, praise God for his blessings, praise Him for His many mercies to you in the past, and thank Him for His faithfulness in the face of your faithlessness.

62 - *Wandering*

Wandering as Pilgrimage
by Diane Boleyn

Psalm 84:5-7 (NIV)
Blessed are those whose strength is in you,
whose hearts are set on pilgrimage. . .
They go from strength to strength, till each appears before God in Zion.

Several years ago after listening to my enthusiastic sales pitch, my husband decided to forego his annual fall fishing trip to Northern Minnesota to wander with me.

For some time, I had been dreaming of the ultimate road trip – following the Mississippi River on the Great River Road. From beginning to end. Down one side. Up the other. We've heard that the trip can be made in 36 hours - straight through. Or, in 4-10 days at a little slower clip. In our case, the trip will take several years. Bit by bit. As we have time. As we have money. As our family situation and ministry responsibilities will allow.

And so far, I have to confess, we've not gotten far – Minnesota. Iowa. Northern Illinois. We are perfecting this wandering pilgrimage. We're not lost, just on an adventure of discovery and growth.

As we followed our maps and the GPS, we meandered with the river, sometimes only dimly aware of its presence hidden by bluffs. The river, even out of sight, still dominated our route.

Occasionally the map and the road signs haven't agreed. There have been detours. We've slogged through miles at speeds of 25-30 miles per hour, surrounded by houses and heavy traffic.

We've also been on remote roads, going hours without seeing another person or car.

Shortly after we began the first leg of this pilgrimage, we realized that if our goal was to complete a portion on a schedule we would have to scuttle all sight-seeing not directly connected to the river.

We planned one day at a time, researching as we went along.

So far, our trip journal is filled with random notes about unexpected finds, frustrations, questions, and joys.

I like to think that the Psalmist's pilgrimage to Jerusalem was filled with some of the same challenges we experience as we wander on the Great River Road.

In a similar sense God has called us to make an intentional pilgrimage with him throughout our lives. He has not promised that our journey will be straight, easy, and fast.

In fact, he asks us to slow down in order to pay attention to him and discern his presence even when it is not obvious. He invites us to wander with him, to listen for his voice, and to experience our faith journey as an adventure of discovery and growth. He asks us to set aside distractions that keep us from pilgrimage and focus on today – this moment.

Because he travels with us, detours and disappointments will help us go from strength to strength.

Jesus, you are the Way, the Truth, and the Life. Continue to strengthen and encourage us as we wander with you along the way of spiritual pilgrimage and growth.

Sept. 24, 2016

Oct. 5, 2017

July 19, 2024

Wandering Broken in the Wilderness
by Mike DeLong

Mark 1:12-13 (NLT)
The Spirit then compelled Jesus to go into the wilderness,
where he was tempted by Satan for forty days.
He was out among the wild animals, and angels took care of him.

Craaaack! And just like that, my bone was broken.

Happily serving as one of the camp pastors that week, I had planned a simple "Jesus in the Wilderness" re-enactment; you know, I hide behind a small bush on the opposite side of Village Creek, wait until the singing was done, and then emerge dressed as the Lord Jesus, ready to face the Tempter who was carefully (and safely, I might add) hiding up in the trees above the chapel. I'd earlier found a fairly smooth place in the creek to wade across, and it was, after all, pretty shallow.

Stepping out of the water, I was below the embankment, unseen now until I would crest the top. As I felt my body going out from under me, I held more tightly to the walking stick and tried to jam my right foot into the soil of the hillside. The soil didn't move; but the first metatarsal on my right foot did - in a way it wasn't intended to move! And just like that, my bone was broken.

"Now what?" I said to myself, face down in the dirt, with every nerve in my foot screaming in pain. Temptations flooded in - complain, give up, fail.

"Do I stop the chapel and head to the nurse's office? Do I keep going in spite of the pain? What will the campers think? And, oh yea, what about Satan up there in the trees, waiting on my appearance?"

In the anxious few seconds I felt God's Peace settle over me - right there in the "wilderness" of Village Creek, with the enemy waiting in the trees, and lots of eyes and hearts watching from their benches. I sensed the Lord's Presence in those moments, sensed that while, I was now wandering broken, I wasn't wandering alone in the wilderness.

"Mike, I'm here for you right now. Your bone, and maybe your pride, have suffered a bit of a break, but I got you; I'm right here. And I've got all those campers up there; and truth be told, I got that enemy up there too."

With His help, and I believe an angel or two, we completed the chapel. Most importantly, we proclaimed God's Word - real and true.

Brokenness can happen at any time; and wandering in the wilderness can happen wherever you are. God is right there with you; the Lord knows about wandering.

There will come a time, in the wandering that we all must do as we seek His Kingdom, that we will find ourselves broken. And in those times of brokenness, we may be tempted to complain, or give up, and just settle for failure.

But know this - Jesus has been in the wilderness; He knows what it means to wander. And the Lord knows what it means to have angels take care of Him.

Do not quickly reject brokenness and wandering. The brokenness we experience may one day be one of the many gifts God desires us to use for His Glory.

Father of All Who Wander and All Who are Broken, please help me to know Your Presence in my pain and in my wandering. Assure me that your ministering angels are there as they were for Jesus. And fill me with fresh courage and strength to get up & go on in ministry for Your Glory!

Sept. 27, 2016
Sept. 21, 2017
July 19, 2024

A Wanderer Finds His Bearings
by Pastor David Dryer

Psalm 119:10, 21 (ESV)
With my whole heart I seek you;
let me not wander from your commandments!
You rebuke the insolent, accursed ones,
who wander from your commandments.

There is very little in life I enjoy more than wandering the state of Wisconsin on my Harley Sportster. Heading west into the unknown with an unplanned itinerary is the epitome of joy! And it is always west – because I live on the eastern border of Wisconsin which happens to be a very large body of water known to us as Lake Michigan.

So west it is, always vigilant for roads I've never been down. Scattered throughout our state are specially marked roads labeled "Rustic Roads" -- roads that bring nature's scenery right up to the shoulder. On many of them, the trees on each side meet over the road creating a natural canopy. Wandering down those roads is always invigorating, even when I have no idea where I might be.

Fortunately I have a good sense of direction. Getting lost while wandering is not something I worry about. And one of the big reasons is that great big lake which makes up the eastern border of my state.

If I thought I was lost, just head east! If I'm riding in the morning, head for the sunrise! If I'm riding in the afternoon, head away from the sunset! If it is high noon, stop at a McDonalds for a milkshake and wait for the sun to begin its journey toward the west! No matter where my wandering may take me, I can always depend on Lake Michigan being to my east. Make it back to the lake and you'll have your bearings to guide you home.

The Psalmist understood this concept when applied to our lives as we follow Jesus Christ. His "Lake Michigan" was the Scriptures, God's Word, the Holy Bible. He recognized that in wandering, for whatever reason, he might be tempted to take his eyes off his God. So he prayed fervently, *"Let me not wander from your commandments! May my life at all times be immersed in the Word of God!"* Why did he pray this way? Because he knew that God speaks clearest to his people through the Scriptures. No matter where he was, no matter where he wandered, no matter what the circumstances – God would meet him there.

And what was true for the psalmist is still true for you. Whether you wander for fun, or, you've wandered in confusion or sin, God is waiting to meet with you in His Word. Cultivating the daily habit of reading the Scriptures will give you the bearings you need to guide you where God wants you to be.

Lord, "I will meditate on your precepts and fix my eyes on your ways. I will delight in your statutes, I will not forget your word. My tongue will sing of your word, for all your commandments are right." Psalm 119:15-16, 172(ESV)

It Seemed Plain, But...
by Jay Fruechte

Jonah 1:1-3a (ESV)

Now the word of the LORD came to Jonah,
saying, "Arise, go to Nineveh, that great city,
and call out against it, for their evil has come up before me."
But Jonah rose to flee to Tarshish from the presence of the LORD.

Many of us wish we could know exactly what God wants for us and for our lives. I've wanted the same thing, but of course it didn't change Jonah. A few years ago, I was in a dark place and instead of seeking God and his will in my life, I decided to seek escape.

The date was set for my Brazilian study abroad. At the end of July, I would leave my family, friends, and all accountability for 6 months to do whatever I wanted. Though I wanted to be apart from God, I would soon learn that it's more about what He wants.

The day I left America for Brazil was a day of tears and smiles, entrapment and escape, rebellion, and ultimately a turn for sanctification.

My parents dropped me off at Cedar Rapids Airport, and I made the plane with about 3 minutes to spare. As the plane took off, and I looked down on the lusciously green fields of corn and soybeans of Iowa, I realized this would be the last time I would see Iowa for 6 months, the longest I had ever been from home. Something wasn't right, it hit me that I left home wanting sin, but God wanted something different for me. This sequence can best be described by the flights I took.

- **CID to ATL**: I, for whatever reason, put on a sermon which happened to be over Ephesians 5, which happened to talk about all the evils that I wanted to participate in, which happened to convict my heart and make me realize that loving Him was so much better.

- **ATL to GRU**: I was crossing borders now. Everything I wanted to do was now taboo. This plane ride was full of worry, discouragement, and fear. I thought the next 6 months would be full of loneliness and despair for punishment.
- **GRU to GYN**: My spot on the plane was next to a dad and his 2 year old daughter. I thought, "Oh great! Crying for three hours, just what I needed for an already stressful day. As you would have it this was God's first big act of providence for me in Brazil. This man was a missionary going to visit his father and brother. These men, along with their wives and children, became Christian guides and friends to me.

In less than 12 hours, my grand plans of walking away from God were destroyed by some stellar teaching, emotion, and ultimately by Him.

Having a missionary contact and a heart change was only the beginning. I soon met Christian friends, people to minister to, I was met with a sovereignty that saved me from countless dangerous situations, and the love of a Father that gives peace and joy.

Jonah's running away is only the beginning of the story. God still uses him despite all of his weaknesses and his eagerness to wander. It wasn't about Jonah; it was about God and His mission, and God will always accomplish His Mission.

Lord, let me forget myself and my desires, and let me seek You and what You desire.

Wandering about (in) Church
by Rev. Cole Griffin

Luke 24:32 (ESV)
They said to each other, "Did not our hearts burn within us while he talked to us on the road, while he opened to us the Scriptures?"

I'll never forget his words, "I'm coming after you."

What I thought was going to be a pleasant pastoral conversation with a leader in the church turned out to be a war cry. Totally blind-sided by words of attack, condemnation and accusations, ending the conversation with a pastoral prayer did not seem appropriate. During this impromptu meeting after church services, I was informed that I was a heretic, deceptive and had secret plans to convert our church congregation into a New Age cult!

While these accusations and assumptions were all untrue, the artillery campaign of shock and awe to "come after me" wrought its damage on my friendships, my morale, but perhaps most importantly my own soul. Church can be a contact sport, often without the decorum displayed even in a neighborhood pick-up basketball game. We don't often talk about the topic of church hurt, but it's real. It's been said before that Christians are the only army in the world where its own soldiers shoot each other.

Having to work through this very difficult circumstance with someone that I had trusted and yes even admired, caused me to dig deeper into my own understanding of walking with Christ. I found myself floating for a while, seemingly unmoored from the safe docks of all my good theology and rational thought.

It was a strange feeling to feel kind of lost and wandering about in my own church setting – not understanding why I had been so targeted while trying to serve the people that I loved.

I began to slowly realize that my experience is not all that different from the crew who followed Jesus in person 2000 years ago. In the aftermath of the crucifixion and all the pain and confusion that ensued, many of the Christ's followers found themselves wandering a bit until they could get their bearings again with The Truth.

Consider the tender story in Luke 24:13-35. One of the most beautiful passages in the Bible, we see Jesus (hiding his identity from the two walkers) taking the time to walk with his two followers who were utterly bereft and confused post-crucifixion. The reality of the resurrection had not made its way through the rank and file of Christ's followers. As Cleopas and another unnamed disciple walked along the road to Emmaus, trying to make sense of what had happened, they encountered the living Christ who took the time to listen to their pain and confusion. Then Jesus breaks bread with them and their hearts burned in his presence. Even those who walked with Christ during his earthly ministry found themselves confused and hurt.

Have you ever found yourself wandering about in your church setting after a difficult conversation or encounter with a fellow Christian? Do you find yourself in a place of cynicism and bitterness when you think of your church leaders? Perhaps Jesus is calling you to take a walk with him today. Let him unfold the scriptures in your heart to bring healing and grace. The truth and power of the resurrection has the power to win the battle raging inside of your soul. Be encouraged today that Jesus is walking with you and even though other Christians may hurt you (they are on their own journey too), Jesus is the one who can turn your wandering into a direct path to spiritual transformation.

Lord Jesus, while I'm prone to wander I know that you want to walk with me, even in my own places of confusion and disillusionment. Help me to give you access to the places in my own soul that need the truth of the Gospel. And Lord, please show me the way so that I don't get lost in my own pain. May it be so.

A Light in the Dark
by Mark Jaspers

John 1:5 (MSG)
The Life-Light blazed out of the darkness;
the darkness couldn't put it out.

Not all who wander are lost. As a free spirit who has been bitten by the travel bug I can certainly relate to this adage. Having inherited my grandfather's directional savvy and love of exploring I have enjoyed the spontaneity and adventure of wandering *sans* fear of being lost in the proximal-directional sense.

Depression has been a part of my journey since middle school. For me, it's a struggle wrought with periods of inner darkness – often intense – sometimes quite lengthy – in which I have felt utterly lost. In these moments a different form of wandering takes place where I have no sense of direction, nor do I find it easy to identify any semblance of light during the darkest moments. It's suffocating and overwhelming. And, at times, entirely terrifying and crippling.

I did get lost once a couple of years ago, ironically on a soul-searching trip during a particularly intense period of depression. One afternoon I decided to venture down a slightly-worn path through a forest of trees hundreds of years old, crying out to God and asking him to grant even a piece of clarity or confidence that he was, indeed, real.

While walking I found the trail growing narrower, winding and curving, while the trees converged closer together, creating a thick canopy above that allowed very little light in.

My usual, trusted inner-compass had failed and as the afternoon sun waned I realized I was entirely lost. Proximally. Emotionally. Spiritually.

It was in that looming darkness and holistic weariness I had my Jonah-in-the-belly-of-the-fish-epiphany.

Recalling scripture about God turning darkness to light (II Sam. 22:29) and Christ IS light so I can walk with him (I Jn. 1:5&7), I began to discover truths I had been taught as if seeing them again for the first time.

This depression piece is a piece of me; it is part of my humanity, yet it doesn't have to own or overpower me. An emotional deficit is one way my weakness (and subsequent need for Christ) allows for the Lord's strength to empower me (II Cor. 12:9-10).

I wish I could tell you that each of my personal experiences with depression bouts provides/allows for this glorious beam-of-Heaven's-light wisdom nugget; it's not always the case.

I still have moments of searching, calling out, and the tendency to wander along depression's dark paths, moments when I struggle with questions and doubts. But then I try remembering the lessons learned in my own wandering. I find comfort in the privilege we each have to know, in part, the mystery of the God-man, Jesus Christ.

Even when the answers aren't clear, even when the stormy clouds of depression circle overhead, even when I am searching to see even a pinhole of light blazing through dark surroundings, I know I am invited to search for (and find) the Light that shines in/overcomes all darkness.

Father God, thank you for being with me as I search and find you. Guide me and direct me in this mystery.

Oct. 24, 2016

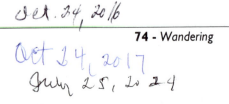

Unlikely Guide in an Unexpected Place
by Harrison Lippert

Psalm 139:9-10 (NIV)
If I rise on the wings of the dawn, if I settle on the far side of the sea, even there your hand will guide me, your right hand will hold me fast.

In February of 2003, a plane flew across the Atlantic overnight into the dawn taking me away from my wife and then six children to settle on the far side of the sea in a remote peninsula of a country named Qatar. My settling spot was the bottom bunk in a long row of bunk beds, one of three long rows in a large perpetually dark tent, one of several tents set up on the concrete floor under the shelter of a warehouse, one of several large tan warehouses set up in rows that made up Camp As Sayliyah. Central Command Headquarters forward base to coordinate Operation Iraqi Freedom.

In early January, while in my associate pastor office at church, a mobilization officer called requesting I volunteer for activation as a staff chaplain for Central Command. I had just completed a several month online course required for future promotion entitled, Air Command and Staff College.

During the course I joked with my wife, Pam, "What does an Air National Guard chaplain in South Dakota need to know about a Marine Joint Task Force?" No one was joking now. After discussing the request with her, with the church leadership and with my parents, the guidance was clear to go and serve.

I imagined an exciting tour of duty, choppering over and around the enemy into small forward operating bases to bring life-giving ministrations.

The night to night routine in Camp As Sayliyah proved less dramatic. As the night shift chaplain, I visited the various areas of the base and made some good friendships. I led a small worship service for night shift workers at 3 AM. I helped some lonely and hurting people. My most exciting and dangerous moment involved a *colorful* tongue-lashing from the command chaplain for loaning out *his* SUV to another office.

During my night walks and morning returns to and from my bunk, surrounded by brown in the day or under the beautiful Arabian night sky, I would often whistle, *He Leadeth Me.*

That song just echoed through my mind. When given the option to cap my tour at 90 days or extend for a year, God's leading was clear. Someone else can have this opportunity. My family needs me and I them. One concern now--during that flight into the dawn was, I had resigned from my church. A couple days before my return the relief chaplain came and we traveled the base talking about God's leading.

We stepped onto one of the buses that made routes on the base. I was overheard sharing my employment concern by another lone passenger. The soldier turned to me and with a confident, almost chiding tone assured me that God had called me here and would certainly take care of me on my return.

Wherever your wandering may take you, be assured that God's right hand will hold you fast and his reassuring voice will guide you.

Lord keep me listening for your voice to guide me in my wanderings. Remind me that you may speak from unlikely people in unlikely places.

Needing a Daily Practice
by Sue Lyford

2 Peter 3:17-18 (ESV)
You therefore, beloved, knowing this beforehand, take care that you are not carried away with the error of lawless people and lose your own stability. But grow in the grace and knowledge of our Lord and Savior Jesus Christ. To him be the glory both now and to the day of eternity. Amen.

I want to be an artist. I want to sketch, draw, and paint. I was organizing my craft closet the other day. I have all the supplies – a sketch pad, charcoal pencils, paint brushes, canvas... I have all I need (some would say I have too much!). I can whip them out at any time and put ink – paint – pencil – on paper or canvas. I can envision what I want to create and how I want to fashion it. The shades of gray charcoal, short swift marks and thin delicate lines coordinating into a complete picture; the bold colors of oil paint – a little dense at times to add texture, combining and blending together to create new colors that no one has ever encountered.

I even have books that teach me how to be a better artist – how to use those supplies and materials to create beautiful things. And don't get me started on Pinterest ideas...

But I can't paint. I can't sketch, and I can't draw anything. My problem isn't poor intentions; my problem is that I don't practice. I don't spend time with my pencils, or paints, or canvas. I have dreams and aspirations but because I am not consistent, the final product that I desire is not a part of my life.

If I were to practice a little, I would get a little better at painting and drawing. Imagine what could happen if I practiced a lot?

And then I realized... the same is true with my relationship with God.

I believe the Word of God is Truth (2 Timothy 3:16), and that knowing God's Word is a vital part of knowing the character of God.

I have the Book — several versions in fact. NIV, ESV, NASB, the Message, NKJV... you name it and it's probably on my shelf, coffee table, or night stand. Jesus is my Savior and knowing (and loving) His character compels me to be more like Him in my actions and my deeds.

Imagine if I used the Bible like I use my art supplies! If I didn't spend time reading God's Word, praying, and working to improve my relationship with my Heavenly Father, I would be lost!

My flesh would make poor choices and I would depend on my own stability (not a good idea!). Reading His Word <u>daily</u> allows me to stand grounded in Him <u>daily</u>. The Word of God is vital to growing in grace and to bringing Him glory.

Having it in my closet (and organizing it on the shelves) doesn't help me, but getting it out and using it will improve my life drastically.

What's keeping you from reading the Bible today?

Lord, help me to prioritize time with You each day and to know You better so I can be more like You.

Confession Between the Trees
by Bryce Roskens

I John 1:9 (NLT)
But if we confess our sins to him,
he is faithful and just to forgive us our sins
and to cleanse us from all wickedness.

I grew up with a fairly large backyard. On one side of the yard were two parallel rows of trees. These trees were important in my childhood.

My older brother, who is three years older than I am, has always been bigger and stronger. When we were kids, I had a pretty bad habit of being unkind to my older brother. I would intentionally annoy him, do mean things to him, and would often times call him rude and derogatory names. I knew how to push just the right buttons, as any little brother can. But once I pushed that button, there was no going back. If Mom wasn't around, I could only do one thing: RUN FOR MY LIFE!

That's when those rows of trees became my friends. I would zig-zag back and forth around those trees to avoid the oncoming retaliation. I was faster, so I could always escape, for a period of time at least. As I wove through the trees, my stamina slowly diminished as the gap between my brother and me disappeared. In those closing moments, I would yell out in a frantic voice, "I'm sorry! I didn't mean it! I'll do whatever it takes to make it right." And then he pounced.......

I wasn't really sorry. I just didn't want the cruel and unusual big brother punishment to begin. I clearly confessed my wrongdoing to my brother, but he wasn't interested in hearing it. In this involuntary surrender, confession was fake, shallow, and self-serving.

For years in my Christian journey, I've wondered about confession. What's the purpose? What good does it do? God knows my failures and my wrongdoings. Why do I need to repeat and vocalize these mistakes to Him?

God cares about our relationship with Him. Thankfully, God's not an angry big brother who clobbers us and refuses to listen to our confessions. He willingly forgives wrongdoing because His Son died on a tree as a perfect sacrifice for sin, but we must confess honestly to claim that forgiveness. We must turn to God as Lord and Savior. Just like in a healthy marriage or friendship, confession is an act of humility and shows a desire to be in right relationship. When's the last time you've been open and honest with God in confession? Wherever you find yourself today, don't miss an opportunity to confess to a loving God.

God, humble me. Help me take the sin in my life seriously today. Let nothing get in the way of my relationship with you. When I fall short, help me to be open and honest with you because you are the sustainer of our relationship. Heavenly Father, help my confession of sin today lead to a greater obedience and closeness to you. Amen.

Nov. 3, 2016
July 28, 2024

We Hear His Voice
by Cindy Schwerdtfeger

John 10:3 (ESV)
The sheep hear his voice,
and he calls his own sheep by name and leads them out.

When I was young and got lost in the store, my mom would quack like a duck so that my brother and I would hear her voice and come back to her. She said it was because she was the momma duck and we were her little ducklings. It sounds corny but it was a tactic that worked because we were comforted by her familiar voice and we would come running to be by her side.

As my kids got older and would tend to run off in the store and get lost, I told my husband what my mom did and that we should do something similar so the kids could find us. We were talking about it with the kids, and no one was excited about duck noises as "our sound." We talked about different options but nothing sounded like the best one.

Then we remembered that we had just seen the movie, *Iron Will*, and there was a sound in that movie that could be used – Will's distinctive whistle. In the movie, Will Dodd enters a dog sled race in his now-deceased father's place to save the farm.

Will uses his dad's famous whistle to get the attention of the lead sled dog, Gus, to spur him on. Everyone agreed to use this whistle and it actually worked!

When one of the kids was lost in a store, we'd whistle and then we'd hear, "I'm over here, Mom" or "I am coming, Dad." I don't ever remembering anyone around us being upset that we were whistling in the store or asking us why we were doing that. Whatever the case, it always worked and our kids were relieved when they found us shortly after hearing the whistle.

Similarly, sheep often wander off and can get lost. They will blindly follow the other sheep and get into trouble. The sheep will bleat and bleat, calling out for the shepherd. The shepherd finds them and leads them to safety. We are similar to the sheep that get lost or distracted by things around us. We make choices that lead us down a wrong path and we need the Savior's help.

John 10:3 says, *"The sheep hear his voice, and he calls his own sheep by name and leads them out."* We just need to call out for the Savior's help. When we hear His voice calling our name, we need to run back into His arms. His voice will comfort us, wherever we are, and He will lead us to safety.

What about you? Are you lost and wandered off from the Savior? Is it time for you to call Him and listen for His voice?

Lord, I have wandered from you and am lost. Please rescue me and take me back to the safety of Your arms. Amen.

Nov. 4, 2016
Oct. 31, 2021
July 30, 2024

Questions to Consider/Discuss

1. When you read the hymn that opened this section, what reaction(s) did you have to it?

2. When you read the hymn's author's background, what thoughts did you have about that person's life, circumstances, or character?

3. What entries from this section were the most helpful to you?

4. What Scripture(s) did you find surprising to see in this section?

5. How were you encouraged in this section of the book?

6. What challenges or encouragements would you like to incorporate into your life after reading this section?

7. What is one change you intend to make based on the readings in this section?

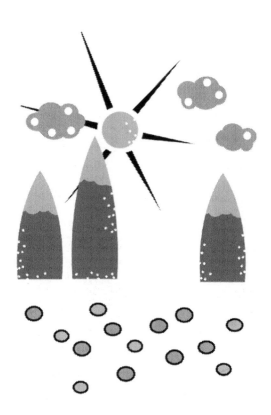

Joy to the world, the Lord is come!
Let earth receive her King;
Let every heart prepare Him room,
And heav'n and nature sing,
And heav'n and nature sing,
And heav'n, and heav'n, and nature sing.

Joy to the earth, the Savior reigns!
Let men their songs employ;
While fields and floods, rocks, hills, and plains
Repeat the sounding joy,
Repeat the sounding joy,
Repeat, repeat, the sounding joy.

No more let sins and sorrows grow,
Nor thorns infest the ground;
He comes to make His blessings flow
Far as the curse is found,
Far as the curse is found,
Far as, far as, the curse is found.

He rules the world with truth and grace,
And makes the nations prove
The glories of His righteousness,
And wonders of His love,
And wonders of His love,
And wonders, wonders, of His love.[4]
Isaac Watts

Hymn Reflection: Joy
by Jen Woyke

Isaac Watts grew up in a church where the only songs sung in worship were psalms. In the early 1700's as he was hitting adulthood, Isaac, struggled with the "incompleteness" of singing Psalms that spoke of joy but only hinted at the source of our joy--Christ. Watts sought to remedy that with this song based on the second half of Psalm 98.

Psalm 98 and the theme of joy is an interesting topic for Watts to write about. You see, he struggled most of his adult life with significant depression. His mental state was so debilitating that he suffered a nervous breakdown in 1712 and was unable to consistently preach at the church he pastored or even live by himself. He moved in with friends and lived with them until his death 36 years later. So how did this man write one of the most quintessential hymns on joy in the English language? I think it's because he saw the TRUTH. Christ IS the source of our joy as believers...not our circumstances...not our families...not our friends or accomplishments or stuff...and not our mental state...

The joy that this hymn speaks of is not a feeling...it's knowledge. It's truth. The Lord has come. Christ wants to be Lord of our lives. He has saved us. Our joy, in the most real sense possible, springs from the knowledge that Jesus died on a cross for our sins and he wants us to live in that victory. It's truth that we need to speak into our lives and the lives of others on a daily basis. Allow this hymn to speak truth to you today. Joy to the world, the Lord is come!

Nov. 10, 2016

88 - *Joy*

Joy in an Unlikely Moment
by Jane Kramer

1 Thessalonians 3:20 (ESV)
For you are our glory and joy.

Joy exists at some of the most unlikely times. It can even be present just when we think our world is about to come crashing down or when things look their darkest. It comes in the form of a smile on a grandchild's face, in contentment of a season, and in knowing that our Creator is all-powerful in any situation.

God has given me great joy as He has demonstrated his power through the years in amazing ways. One of those was through the life of my mom - a woman who had an amazing testimony of a life lived with love and grace.

My mom developed multiple sclerosis when she was in her early forties. It was at a time when a lot of experimental drugs were being tested in an attempt to treat this disease, and she went through some very difficult years as she took part in experimental trial treatments. By the age of 61 my mom required full time care due to her MS and due to cancer that had also begun to deteriorate her life. It had become increasingly impossible for her to remain at home. It was a pretty dark time for my dad and our family.

One morning when I went to spend time with her she said, "Suzie, (my nick name), I'm going home today." I replied, "Oh, mom I wish you could, but that just can't happen." But she kept repeating it and telling me about the beautiful light that was just behind me.

My mom looked so radiant that day; her face looked beautiful and her smile so content. She looked liked the mom I knew who had entertained endless birthday parties and Sunday school parties at our home.

This was my mom who read Bible stories to us at bedtime. She looked like the mom I knew who took meals or other items to comfort neighbors or others in times of need. She looked beautiful; she was full of joy.

How could she look this way with all she had endured?

After a lengthy visit I drove home and as I walked into the house the phone was ringing. My mom was right. She was going home. She radiantly walked into the arms of her Savior that day. I realized her beauty and joy all along had come from her relationship with Jesus Christ. You see, Jesus Christ our Lord and Savior is the master over all of creation and He allowed me the privilege to see on that day one of His most beautiful displays of His glory – welcoming a loved one home to live with Him for all eternity.

Even though my heart felt grief, I had a deep joy because I knew that my mom had begun experiencing a life of wonder with Jesus that day. He is our glory and the giver of ultimate joy.

Dear LORD help me to remember that true joy comes from knowing you – that is deeper than the "stuff" of this world. Help me to see you on difficult days. Thank you for loving me and allowing me to see the works of your hands.

My Heart Leaps for Joy
by Joanna Lerud

Psalm 28:7 (NIV)
Praise be to the Lord, for he has heard my cry for mercy. The Lord is my strength and my shield; my heart trusts in him, and I am helped. My heart leaps for joy and I will give thanks to him in song.

My fifty fashion design students and I took a much-anticipated field trip to a local mall. The goal of the trip was for each of the students to buy fabric for their sewing project. More than two hours later, the mission was almost accomplished!

Forty-eight students were loaded back on the bus, and I was preparing to join them, when I received a call from our high school police officer.

"Two of your students got in trouble at the mall. They are with other police officers right now, and they will not be returning back to school with you."

I was shocked, disappointed, and angry.

One week later, I sat across from these girls in a "restorative justice circle." Other staff and I shared how we were negatively impacted by the decisions these girls had made. The girls had an opportunity to ask for forgiveness. We had an opportunity to forgive.

As soon as the girls tearfully shared how sorry they were, I bounded out of my seat to hug them and forgive them. I couldn't wait a second longer to express how I felt and restore our relationship!

Isn't that how God responds to our heartfelt cries for forgiveness? Isn't He just waiting for that moment, so He can embrace us and welcome us back into fellowship with Him?

And there is such a sense of relief and joy when we have been cleansed and forgiven!

Psalm 32:4-5 talks about the guilt of sin. *"For day and night your hand was heavy upon me; my strength was sapped as in the heat of summer. Then I acknowledged my sin to you and did not cover up my iniquity. I said, 'I will confess my transgressions to the Lord' —and you forgave the guilt of my sin."*

I love how the Psalmist responds to that forgiveness, "My heart leaps for joy!"

That's how I feel when I'm forgiven and also when I offer forgiveness.

Wouldn't this be a great day to ask for forgiveness, restore a relationship with someone else or with God, and feel your heart "leap for joy"?

Lord, thank you for hearing my cry for mercy. Thank you for forgiving my sin. Thank you for the joy that follows forgiveness!

INFJOY
by Janis Marks

Romans 8:28 (NLT)
And we know that God causes everything to work together for the good of those who love God and are called according to his purpose for them.

Several years ago, I opted to have my license plates personalized. The vehicle itself is tired and worn. It has clearly travelled some difficult roads.

The vehicle has travelled some difficult roads by carrying my precious family through our daily lives. My husband and I have travelled through deep waters in caring for our girls. We have seen our daughters fight for survival and have witnessed miracles. We grieve what they have lost and what they may never be able to experience.

When we renew our plates each year a portion of the fee goes to the Children's Hospital of Wisconsin Trust Fund. We have spent weeks, actually months there with both of our daughters as they have struggled to be where they are today. In the midst of everything, we still find joy. Infinite Joy!

INFJOY

If you would have seen me travelling down the road in our worn out Chevy Astro Van with 238,000 miles on it with these special plates, what would you think it meant?

My friends, in the lowest valley, the deepest pit or the enormous victory at the mountain top, God is there with you. There is no such thing as perfection in this life, but He is able to bring joy in all circumstances because of His presence.

We need to stop looking at others' lives and wishing that their road was our road. It is so easy to look at someone else's life. We may long for what they have because in our perspective it seems easier. We all have struggles. They just look different.

Greater things are to come. He is preparing you! As we cling to the journey, God can use you no matter where you are in your journey if you seek Him. Pray for wisdom and discernment. He will provide in His perfect timing which may look very different from what we think is perfect.

When we seek joy in our earthly provisions or our circumstances alone we will always be disappointed. The Mighty One is constant. He is faithful.

No matter where you have come from it is not too late. Take the first step. Cry out to Him. He will restore. He will provide even if it is sometimes minute by minute.

Even if your circumstances do not change, He will bring joy. Own that truth, my friends. Praise Him in the storm. Be blessed. Receive what He has for you every morning. In the midst of it all - loss, sorrow, brokenness, pain, triumph, success, and healing - He is there walking with You, holding you, and leading you. We can stand on God's promises that He will never fail us. Because of that promise, we can find joy in the journey.

Blessings to you, my friends, WHEREVER you are in your journey. He will meet you there. Our help comes from the Lord. He is our victor. I pray this day brings you joy! GO!

Faithful Father: thank you for providing joy in our journey. Thank you for being our joy – Infinite Joy!

Jehovah Jireh - the God Who Provides
by Carol Potratz

James 1:2-3 (NIV)
Consider it pure joy, my brothers and sisters,
whenever you face trials of many kinds,
because you know that the testing of your faith produces perseverance.

Suddenly! Instantly! Becoming illiterate is anything BUT easy or fun!! All my life I have enjoyed reading... learning...communicating! So, imagine the difficulty when I went to Japan at 60, to be a missionary!

In Japanese there are 4 different alphabets: *hiragana* (for Japanese words), *katakana* (for foreign words, like my name, Carol キャロル), *kanji* (Chinese characters), *romaji* (Roman letters like ours.)

What a confusing situation! Is it possible to make a difference when the only alphabet I can use is the only one they don't use? How will I be a difference-maker when most Japanese study English but cannot speak it and yet, English is the ONLY language I am fluent in?!

This seemed like an impossible situation, and yet, just before coming to Japan, I had been at Village Creek Bible Camp telling the campers and staff about 'being called by God to do what seems to others to be impossible'! BEING a difference-maker! How ironic, huh? No, how like God!

One of the names of God is Jehovah Jireh – the God who provides. I knew this as I have watched and experienced His provision MANY times. So, as I looked around my neighborhood and began to ponder how God in me could make a difference – in spite of the language situation, I began to see, hear, and experience my surroundings with 'new eyes & new ears.'

Almost immediately, I developed a love for my neighbors and our setting. The Lord began to fill my heart with joy as I walked to work and back each day, meeting folks along the way and stopping by various businesses to greet them! Some days, prompted by God, I would take my neighborhood businesses something baked or something 'special' from North America that family or friends had sent. (They were shocked, and pleased, that I would do that!)

Why did I do that? Notice that I said, 'prompted by God'? Well, this is EXACTLY why I did it! Our God knew my location and the folks who lived there better than I did and He nudged me in some specific ways to meet real needs of real people. Do you think this only happens to missionaries? The answer is "NO!" This kind of wisdom is given to anyone who asks our generous God (vs 5.)

Jehovah Jireh wants to provide for YOU; … in YOUR locality, …through YOUR gifts. He longs to fill YOU with joy so that you'll be stronger in faith and have the ability to be steadfast. He is calling YOU to be a difference-maker.

Jehovah Jireh, you indeed ARE the Provider! Today, give me eyes to see what you see and ears to hear what you hear. Help me to see myself as you do that I might have the confidence to truly ACT on the prompting of your Spirit. Amen.

Joy in the Morning
by Jim Renke

Psalm 30:5 (ESV)
For his anger is but for a moment,
and his favor is for a lifetime.
Weeping may tarry for the night,
but joy comes with the morning.

"Dad, it's not good."

I was trying to hear through the fuzzy bluetooth connection, register what was happening and hurtling down the highway at 75 miles per hour. My oldest son called to give an update on the birth of our first granddaughter, Clara Grace.

We asked what was wrong and through tears, he said, "A lot." Clara was born with arthrogryposis; a name we wouldn't learn until much later. What it meant was that her arms and legs were bent, her joints were tight and constricted. At that moment, breathing was the big concern.

For the next 90 minutes, my wife and I cried, prayed, and hoped. We couldn't imagine the pain our kids were feeling. My anxiety and pain increased as I anguished and rehearsed what life might hold in the days ahead. At the hospital, we heard the updates, and as a family we went into the NICU. I sat in a chair and Andrew handed me his little girl. She seemed half her size. Her legs were bent. Her chin was small. Her arms gripped her torso, unable to stretch. She was a bundle, all balled-up.

I held her, afraid and filled with love. I was also filled with a palpable joy. My tears flowed as I told her again and again that she was loved. God loved her and so did we. Where did the joy come from? It didn't come from empty promises of an easy life. Nor did it come from any knowledge that this would be fixed. It came from getting a glimpse that Clara's story was part of God's story of grace and redemption. The joy came from understanding that the author of all things was writing a story that only Clara could live. And because He's good, her story would be good.

The psalmist wrote, "Weeping may tarry for the night, but joy comes in the morning." Weeping may hang out in darkness, but something happens in the light of day. It doesn't fix things. The light of day brings clarity. It helps us see that God's at work. There is One who is carefully and skillfully crafting a story for us to live with Him. Clara Grace's name means "clear grace." That is what the morning brings, a view of God's clear grace. When we see it we know great joy, even with tears.

Father, thank you for the joy the morning brings. Thank you for the windows through which the light of understanding comes. Thank you for the joy the floods my heart. In every moment of sorrow, or frustration today, help me wait with you for the clarity only You can give. And in this glimpse fill me with unending joy! In Christ's name and for your glory! Amen.

Dec. 3, 2016
Aug 5, 2024

Trusting the Truth
by Alyssa Rubio

Isaiah 40:13-14 (ESV)
Who has directed the spirit of the Lord, or as His counselor has taught him?
With whom did he take counsel, and who instructed him,
who taught him the path of justice?
Who taught him knowledge, and showed him the way of understanding?

Have you ever considered someone to be the "cool" member of your family? Maybe it was a brother, cousin, or uncle? My aunt Lisa was the "cool aunt." When I was younger she would always ask me about life. She was the one I felt I could trust with my precious teenage secrets. She also loved the Lord with her whole heart and motivated me to do the same.

In November of 2007, I was studying at a Bible Institute in Argentina, when I received news from home that after many years of fighting with cancer my aunt Lisa had passed away.

I had the hardest time understanding why. If I´m honest, it's still hard because I can´t find a reason why the Lord would take a person like her from this earth.

After asking God many times the question of, why, I realized that I was holding onto the unknown instead of holding on to the known. I don´t know why God took my aunt to be with him, but I do know who God is! This verse in Isaiah shows us just one of the many characteristics of God. God is omniscient which means that he knows everything.

No one ever gave him advice or told him what decision to make; he is the all-knowing God! And because he is perfect in wisdom, he will never be wrong and never make a mistake. That is what I cling to.

There are going to be questions in life that we aren´t going to have the answers for. I find joy in remembering that the all-knowing God of wisdom is in control. My heart still hurts when I think of my aunt, but it is so much easier when I don´t question his infinite wisdom but trust him.

Maybe you are aching inside, and all want you is for the Lord to take that pain from you. Trust that he is all-knowing and that his plan is perfect no matter how much it hurts. He will redeem all things in his mysterious way.

Jesus, help us not to question you but to trust you even in the hard times. May we remember that this world is not our home and may we find joy in you alone and never in our circumstances.

God Knows Your Name

by Molly Sanborn

Psalm 139:17-18 (NLT)

How precious are your thoughts about me, O God. They cannot be numbered! I can't even count them; they outnumber the grains of sand! And when I wake up, you are still with me!

Quite by accident, I fell in love with the name Poppy Joy for our first baby. When I downloaded a pregnancy app on my phone, it notified me: "your baby is 4 weeks old and is the size of a poppy seed."

What started as a cute nickname turned into my all time favorite name for our unborn baby girl. The only problem was that my husband, Craig, was not at all on board.

"That's ok," I thought, "I will pray!" Instead of nagging my husband, I nagged God!

As we prepared for an upcoming trip to Scotland, I prayed that we would meet someone named Poppy while we were there but didn't share that prayer with Craig or anyone else.

Three days into our trip, we drove through a quaint little village and noticed a sign that read "Poppy's Coffee Shop"!

Craig slammed on the breaks, and I bolted out of the door to check it out. My heart sank as I read the closed sign hung on the door and realized I would never know who this Poppy is. My belly, now the size of a small pumpkin, posed for a picture by the sign. I also shared with Craig about my secret prayer to meet a Poppy.

We returned to our lodging later that night. The next morning as we checked out, we chatted with Doug (the owner) in the kitchen. I asked if he could think of any places along our route where there would be poppy flowers.

As he thought about it, I explained to him my obsession with poppies. I told him it was *just* a nickname, that I actually liked it, but that Craig didn't. He got a smirk on his face and said, "That's interesting because Poppy is our daughter's name."

I was hysterical, and Craig just sat on the stool shaking his head. I told Doug how I had prayed to meet a Poppy and couldn't believe that she was living in the house we had been staying at for 3 days! I begged to meet her, like she was some kind of celebrity. He told me she was 15 and in school for the day.

He went on to tell us the inspiration behind the name. He explained that he grew up in a town an hour north of there and lived next to a sweet older lady named Poppy. She was so kind and loving that he had dreamed of naming a daughter after her. "Oh, and that town named a coffee shop after her," he nonchalantly shared.

I hardly had time to react before he went on to tell us that her middle name is Joy! I was so excited I was afraid I'd go into labor right there! When we got in the car, I HAD to know what Craig was thinking. He simply said, "It's not like God is saying it's *ok* to name her Poppy Joy. It's like He's saying her name *is* Poppy Joy."

Each time I reflect on that story, I shake my head in wonderment as I remember that my God is so intimately acquainted with each one of us. He knows the number of hairs *on* our heads (Luke 12:7) and thoughts *in* our heads (Psalm 139:2). He takes such delight in hearing from us and going above and beyond in answering our prayers (Ephesians 3:20). Wherever you are in life, wherever you go – He sees you, He calls you, and He knows your name.

Dear Lord, You know my name and you know everything about me – and Your thoughts toward me are precious. Thank you!

5:36 AM
by Briana Sauder

Ephesians 3:18 (NLT)
And may you have the power to understand, as all God's people should, how wide, how long, how high, and how deep His love is.

It is not uncommon that the greatest joy I feel in a single day occurs somewhere between the hours of 5 and 7 AM. Now, from a morning person to a most-likely-not-morning-person, I understand that you may find this particularly insane, maybe even slightly offensive—and I don't even drink coffee. *gasp* But by all means, please continue.

I love the still of the morning. I love watching the world hit snooze a few times before it wakes up. I love watching the sunrise—especially in Belize over the Caribbean Sea.

My first week of 2016 was spent serving in Belize with an awesome team of camp staff. We adventured with Jesus all over the country and it was the best thing ever.

I had never seen an ocean before, but it took me exactly point three seconds to fall in love with the Caribbean Sea. Only 24 hours of our trip were spent on San Pedro Island, but it was a moment there that made me never want to go home.

A few of us decided to wake up early to witness what would inevitably be the most breathtaking, picturesque sunrise of our lives. With high expectations and sleep in our eyes, we walked down the boardwalk to the middle of the ocean. The world stood still, the sea untouched. Stars and darkness faded only to expose the massive, ugly clouds that sat directly in front of us completely blocking the pinnacle point of the horizon. Awesome.

Until that point in my life, I had never been mocked by clouds. But that morning, they were saying, "Hah! You'll probably never spend another morning on this island and we're ruining it for you! Go buy a post card since your pictures will be terrible." Seriously, clouds are the worst.

---

103 - *Joy*

So there I sat, on the edge of the boardwalk, my feet dangling above the water as I wrestled with frustration against a mass of condensed vapor. What was supposed to be the perfect morning, the perfect photo-op, the perfect postcard from San Pedro, was the biggest disappointment of 2016. It was January 6th.

I ignored the "sunrise" and started praying. And I couldn't stop. Words flowed into a mess of disconnected poetic phrases as I stared across the sea. My heart was overwhelmed by a God who commands waves to dance and the sun to rise and clouds to move (or not).

Not only was I seeing the ocean for the first time, but a true picture of the love of the Father. The many worship lyrics I had sung mindlessly off a screen for so many years finally held meaning. I've never felt so small, yet so loved by my Jesus. The same God who could palm the ocean was holding my heart...and He's holding yours too. Surrounded by the break of day, the salty air, and a brand new joy, my heart was captured and content. I glanced at the time—5:36 AM—because I never wanted to forget that moment.

Whether you're on an island, eating lunch in the break room, picking up toys for the fifteenth time today, or walking down the halls of your school, you too can feel the same joy I did that day. And it doesn't even have to be morning.

Wherever you are, let your heart be captured by the sweet love of Jesus again and again.

Jesus, thanks for moments that remind me just how much you love me. Even in the midst of crazy days, let me slow down enough to find joy in the little things. Teach my heart to be fully satisfied in you today and every day.

Instagram-Proof Joy
by Bri Simpson

Philippians 4:4, 12-13 (NLT)

Always be full of joy in the Lord. I say it again—rejoice! ...I know how to live on almost nothing or with everything. I have learned the secret of living in every situation, whether it is with a full stomach or empty, with plenty or little. For I can do everything through Christ, who gives me strength.

It's 8 AM, and I'm gleefully screaming the old camp classic, "I've got Joy," while raising the flag. Dew drenches our shoes, as the sun peaks through the clouds. My voice echoes throughout the valley as the campers eagerly join:

> I've got joy down in my heart, deep, deep down in my heart. J-O-Y, down in my heart, deep, deep down in my heart. Jesus put it there, and nothing can destroy, destroy, destroy! I've got joy, down in my heart, deep, deep down in my heart.

Fast forward five years: it's 6 AM, and singing about joy is the <u>last</u> thing from my mind. Despite working all weekend, deadlines loom menacingly. I'm staring down the barrel of a week filled with deadlines. Feeling overwhelmed, I start the day by checking Instagram.

The app opens and images of sun-drenched beaches, mountaineering adventures, and delicious food hit me in the face. I begin to stew: how come these people were able to go off and experience exciting things?

You see, I consider myself a follower of Jesus. As part of that, I know that He has a plan and purpose for wherever I am—be it screaming songs about joy or wrestling with a complicated issue at work. But sometimes, it's easy to look around and think: God, I think You got it wrong. I'm called to love people from a hammock on the beach.

There's an oft-repeated saying around camp that is true in my life, "Comparison is the thief of joy." As soon as we take our eyes off who Christ is, seeds of discontentment spring up. That's probably the reason Paul had to remind the Philippians to always be full of joy—you know, the joy that nothing can destroy (destroy, destroy). We forget. We compare. We get jealous.

Joy does not mean getting what we want; I'm still waiting on my beach vacation. It means recognizing *who* is the source of our joy wherever we are. This joy can only come from Christ and is entirely independent of our circumstances.

So here's a modern interpretation of Philippians 4:12-13: I have learned how to live in a cubicle or on an Instagram-worthy vacation. I have learned the secret of living in every situation, whether there is prestige and good pay, or I'm mired in student loans. For I can do everything through Christ who gives me strength.

Where do you need to be reminded of Christ's never-ending joy in your life?

Jesus, remind us of who you are today. I know you are good. Remind me of your faithfulness. Help me to rejoice, always.

March 1, 2017
Aug. 9, 2024

Where Does My Joy Come From?
by Camie Treptau

Proverbs 8:30-31 (ESV)
And I (wisdom) was daily filled with delight,
rejoicing before him always, rejoicing in his inhabited world
and delighting in the children of man.

I love my kids. I mean I really love them, and I don't want to see them grow up. It has been tough letting one go to college, and getting ready to have the next one graduate with a third child close behind. It is a new book, a sequel, rather than a new chapter because the elements of day to day are all so different.

Where is my joy? Where has my joy come from in these last years of raising children?

In Proverbs 8:30-31, Wisdom is telling us where to find joy. Solomon is writing. God had blessed Solomon with great wisdom (he didn't use it all the time). *Wisdom says, "I was filled with delight day after day, rejoicing always in his presence, rejoicing in his whole world and delighting in mankind."* Wisdom tells us to find great joy and fulfillment in three things: God's presence, the world He created, and mankind.

This is profound and so true. Do you know why my days have been filled with joy over these years of raising kids?

The answer is that I have enjoyed day after day rejoicing in God's presence and sharing Him with my kids, rejoicing in God's amazing creation and sharing the wonder of it all with my kids, and rejoicing in so many amazing people – family, friends, church family, authors, speakers, and sharing them with my kids – and having them share their friends with us too.

This new season may bring some challenges of me letting go. I never said I was good with change, but the truth is I will continue to find great joy in days ahead in my Savior, in His amazing creation, and in the blessing of mankind. God says that children are a blessing from the Lord. They are one blessing, but they are not the only blessing. It is important to keep the whole picture in mind.

God created us for relationship with Him, in His amazing creation, and with others as we continue to bring glory to God and as we point people to Him.

Have you experienced joy recently? Prioritize time with your Savior, time in His creation being in amazing wonder and awe, and time with some people to encourage and spur you on.

It would be wise and would bring joy wherever you are.

Heavenly Father — thank you for being my joy. Thank you for being the source of my joy. Thank you for creating us in relationship with you so that I could experience joy every day. Be with me, care for me, and carry me. Be my joy when the circumstances in my life attempt to steal the joy that I might experience. Reveal the joy that you are when all that I see are shadows that hide the joy you want me to see and experience.

March 4, 2017
Aug 10, 2024

Questions to Consider/Discuss

1. When you read the hymn that opened this section, what reaction(s) did you have to it?

2. When you read the hymn's author's background, what thoughts did you have about that person's life, circumstances, or character?

3. What entries from this section were the most helpful to you?

4. What Scripture(s) did you find surprising to see in this section?

5. How were you encouraged in this section of the book?

6. What challenges or encouragements would you like to incorporate into your life after reading this section?

7. What is one change you intend to make based on the readings in this section?

End Notes

(1) Lowry, Robert. "How Can I Keep From Singing?" Public Domain. 1868.

(2) Ken, Thomas. "Awake, My Soul, and with the Sun." Public Domain. 1674.

(3) Robinson, Robert. "Come, Thou Fount of Every Blessing." Public Domain. 1758.

(4) Watts, Isaac. "Joy to the World." Public Domain. 1719.

Daily Prayer Guide for Summer Camps

As mentioned in the introduction, the inspiration for this devotional guide comes from the summer camp theme of Village Creek Bible Camp. Because it is one of many Bible camps around the world, we wanted to provide readers with a way to daily pray for any camp with which they are affiliated.

Sunday: Pray that the campers who arrive today, and the staff who are working, would be renewed and refreshed by God's Word as it is read and proclaimed throughout the week. Ask God to prepare their hearts so that they would want to know Christ more and more.

Monday: Pray that staff and counselors would be anchored to the truth of the Gospel. Pray that they would be able to communicate that truth in a clear and compelling way to campers.

Tuesday: Pray that the staff, counselors, and campers would see God at work in their lives. Ask Him to open their hearts so that they can see their future in Christ regardless of what their current circumstances may be.

Wednesday: Pray that God would bring to light areas of sin for campers and staff alike. Pray that He would work in mighty ways to make all things new in their lives.

Thursday: Pray for campers as they begin to think about returning home. Pray that they would have strength and courage to take the lessons they are learning home with them and that they would live for Christ in their homes, their schools, and their communities.

Friday: Pray for the staff across the camp, many of whom serve in the background. Ask that God be their sufficiency and joy today. Ask God to remind them that they are called to this place and time for a purpose.

Saturday: Pray for relaxation for the amazing staff who work week after week ministering to campers. Pray that God in His mighty power would bolster their excitement, patience, and energy for the next round of campers.

About the Contributors

Courtney Aronson is a recent graduate of the University of Wisconsin-La Crosse. She is excited to be taking on a year of Bible School in Costa Rica where she'll get to use her Spanish and as she says, "learn the story of the Bible from front to back." Her other writings can be found on her blog at beatsforone.blogspot.com.

Elizabeth Bender is a sophomore at Baylor University in Waco, Texas. She works in the athletic ticket office and takes courses to prepare her to be a Child Life Specialist. Beth grew up attending and then serving at Village Creek Bible Camp.

Kerry L. Bender is a preacher, teacher, and speaker. He is the Director of the Christian Leadership Center and a campus chaplain at the University of Mary in Bismarck, ND. In addition, he is the Teaching Pastor at Bismarck Baptist Church. His interests include the theology of proclamation, bringing the academy into the local church, issues involving science and theology, and ecumenical dialogue. He and his wife (Stacy) are empty-nesters with two adult children, one daughter and one son. You can reach him by email: kerry.l.bender@gmail.com.

Stacy Bender is the dean of students at Crosslake Community High School, an online high school in Minnesota. She also serves as an adjunct professor at the University of Mary in Bismarck, ND. She writes (off and on) a blog: slowingtheracingmind.wordpress.com. She has attended Village Creek for over a decade and is thankful for the impact it has had on her entire family.

Diane Boleyn's first experience at VCBC was in 1976 when her husband was camp pastor for a junior camp. She has actively supported her husband in pastoral ministry and military chaplaincy for 44 years. She is a recovering control-freak. She is a serial blog starter who posts occasionally: letdownthenets.blogspot.com.

R. Lee Boleyn is Senior Pastor at First Baptist Church in Elgin, Iowa, where he has served since December 2002. Previously, he spent 22.5 years in the United States Air Force as a chaplain and also served NAB churches in Arvada, Colorado, and Buffalo Center, Iowa. He directed junior camps during two different summers in the early days of Village Creek Bible Camp (1976 & 1977).

Mike DeLong is the husband of Sue and the father of five, all of whom spent wonderful years at VCBC. A former VCBC summer camp pastor, retreat speaker and board member, Mike now pastors a church in Milwaukee, WI, acts in local theatrical productions, and photographs God's Creation.

Joel Detlefsen is a husband, father, and pastor of Riverview Baptist Church in West St. Paul, Minnesota. He grew up attending Village Creek, and now serves as a chapel speaker on occasion (usually for Junior Camps). He blogs on a regular basis at riverviewbaptist.net.

Abigail Dodds is a stay home wife and mama. She's married to Tom and spends her time caring for their 5 kiddos, tackling Mount St. Laundry, getting to know God in His Word, and occasionally blogging at hopeandstay.com.

Pastor Dave Dryer just retired after serving 35 years as pastor of Immanuel Baptist Church in Kenosha, WI. He has been a family camp speaker at Village Creek, but his best memories from the camp are leadership retreats with the men and women of IBC. And nothing beats early morning devotions at VCBC -- watching the sun rise on God's incredible creation.

Jason Esposito is a husband, father of four and lead pastor at Crossway Church. He received his MRE at Trinity International University and Doctor of Ministry at Bethel University. VCBC is one of his favorite places for the past twenty years. You can listen to Jason's sermons at crosswayc.org.

Jay Fruechte is currently a business analyst at Principal Financial Group in Des Moines, Iowa. He is fresh in the "real world," and finding his way every day. He helps with youth ministry at Cornerstone church in Ankeny, and looks forward to helping with the church's downtown Des Moines plant.

Rev. Cole Griffin has been on staff at Grace Church in Racine, WI, for 20 years, currently in the role of executive pastor. He has a passion to see conflict resolved within the church and loves to see how God redeems conflict in our lives for good. He is a Certified Conciliator™ with Peacemaker Ministries and works throughout the country helping churches resolve conflict.

Dina Hanken is a wife, a mom, and a lover of Jesus. She has been attending Village Creek Bible Camp for 15 years. VCBC has made a huge impact on her family. Dina enjoys writing and speaking to women. More of Dina's writing can be found on her blog: thisanxiousheart.weebly.com.

Lori Hetteen is an artist, illustrator, tulip lover, and black coffee drinker. She accepted Christ in the outdoor chapel at Village Creek Bible Camp as a fifth grader, later got her first job there, and met the guy she would marry in the activity center. VCBC has her heart. She lives in Minneapolis with her husband and four children. You can find her work at www.lorihetteen.com.

Mark Jaspers is on staff at Faith Baptist in Minneapolis, serving in the areas of student and worship ministries. Additionally, Mark co-chairs the North American Baptist (NAB) Student Ministries Committee and is a member of the NAB Executive Committee. Mark enjoys theatre and musical events, group sports, travel, reading, food, and being a proud uncle to the world's cutest nieces and nephew.

Crystal Jolin is a wife and mother of four who recently moved to the home where she grew up. She has attended VCBC since childhood and worked on staff for several years. Crystal has a passion for worship and leading others to the character of God.

Jane Kramer is a speaker for women's conferences, events, and retreats. She and her husband Jim have led several small groups and counsel with married couples. One of Jane's favorite places is VCBC where she enjoys connecting with new and old friends. She loves to see how God encourages, restores, and renews women through His Word. Connect with Jane at email: jkramer@heartofiowa.net for speaking engagements.

Debbi Ladwig is on staff at VCBC. She is mother to two adult daughters and their husbands and "Io-Gram" to five grandchildren. While her primary responsibility at camp is to prepare hearty, healthful meals you'll want to come back for, she also loves to serve up solid Biblical teaching in both oral and written form.

Joanna Lerud is a mom of four, a grandma of five, a high school teacher, and a pastor's wife. Her first visit to VCBC was in 1976 when she spent a month at camp training for God's Volunteers/New Day. VCBC family camp is her family's favorite vacation spot.

Harrison Lippert lives in Steamboat Rock, Iowa with his wife Pam and the youngest four of eight children. Harrison serves Steamboat Rock Baptist Church. VCBC has blessed them in many ways the last 13 years including developing one, two, or three Lipperts as staff every summer since 2007.

Sue Lyford has been on staff at VCBC since 2002 when she graduated from Baylor University. She's a fierce Boston Red Sox fan and dotes on her nieces and nephew as often as possible. In her spare time she raises Yorkie puppies and loves to swing kettle bells. You can reach her at sue@villagecreek.net.

John McNabb is a husband and father of three children and papa to two. He is a pastor in Minnesota and enjoys eating out, walking, hanging out with friends and going to camp. He has been a camp speaker at VCBC for 4 years and loves to tell the junior campers about Jesus!

Hannah Nobles is a passionate follower of Jesus currently living in the heart of Atlanta with her filmmaker husband. Her heartbeat is making disciples of all ages and ethnicities for the glory of God. She is a former camper and staff at Village Creek and loves doing ministry there. She also likes that their canteen always has Pepsi ready for her to consume.

Michelle Pearson - Jesus follower, wife to Ric for 25 amazing years, mom to many beautiful children, friend to so many selfless ladies, ministry leader/teacher to a special group of gals in Oregon, WI and daughter to Todd and Barb Hassemer. VCBC simply rocks on many levels to each member of her family - it's a lifeline!

Carol Potratz grew up on a farm about an hour from VCBC and has prayed for, donated to, attended, worked for, or spoken at VCBC since it began!! Carol is Director of Supervised Ministry and is on faculty at Taylor Seminary in Edmonton, Alberta, Canada. Carol is passionate about: Jesus - knowing Him & helping others to know Him, black coffee, young people, live theatre, nature, her nieces & nephews, art, cooking, and teaching!

Shan Reed is a Jesus-follower who lives in Japan working with the North American Baptist Conference at Komyo Christian Church where she has the privilege of sharing Jesus' love with her Japanese friends. She loves to hang out with friends, bake, read, and sit on the beach. Although she has never been to VCBC, camping ministry was an important part of her childhood.

Jim Renke is Regional Minister of the Upper Mississippi Region of the NAB Conference. He and his wife, Kris, have four sons and one grandchild. Jim has enjoyed serving at Village Creek as camp pastor. Jim's blog can be found at www.jimrenke.com.

Joseph Romeo is pastor of Calvary Baptist Church in Parkersburg, Iowa. He is married to his high school sweetheart, Debra, and they have three children: Anthony, Jacelyn, and Dominick. He blogs at www.jvromeo.wordpress.com.

Bryce Roskens, his wife Amber, and 4 kids live in Iowa. As the youth pastor of Steamboat Rock Baptist Church, he has been pointing teens to Jesus for over a decade, which includes bringing students to VCBC on many occasions. He knows the power of "camp" as he gave his life to Jesus at 11 while attending a Christian camp.

Shane Rothlisberger is the family pastor and finance director at Cornerstone Church of Ames, IA. He grew up attending Village Creek as a camper and served as a counselor for a couple of summers. He and his wife, Michelle, live in Ames with their five children. Follow him on Twitter @pastorshaner.

Alyssa Rubio and her husband Neftali are missionaries in Guadalajara, Mexico through Commission to Every Nation. Alyssa has a passion for seeing youth transformed by the power of the gospel. She attended VCBC from the time she was eight and served several summers on staff.

Molly Sanborn is a wife, mom and speaker. Her life has been forever impacted by Village Creek Bible Camp. She started as a camper, then dishwasher, lifeguard, counselor, and now comes back as a speaker. God wrote Molly and her husband a pretty sweet love story. Check it out at www.CraigandMolly.com.

Briana Sauder: Big fan of Jesus and the Salt Company. Sister to three awesome bros. Daughter to the best parents on the planet. Iowa State Cyclone. Ice cream addict. Lover of cornfields. Probably wearing a flannel. Dream-chaser. Future Physical Therapist. Sometimes she writes: beautifullybroken32.wordpress.com.

Jeannine Sawall is the lucky wife of Marty as well as the blessed mother of four happy, hungry boys. She enjoys coffee with friends, reading, vacations with her family and writing for FreshStart ministries (http://oakwoodfreshstart.blogspot.com). She loves to share the hope only Jesus can give with anyone willing to listen (and sometimes, even those who aren't). She and her family have enjoyed the ministries at VCBC for many years.

Shelly Schmor is a former missionary and is a strong advocate for the role of women within the Kingdom of God. She loves to read, garden, and sit with others over a cup of coffee or tasty beverage, hear their stories, and cheer them on to all that God has for them. She is the proud wife of Randy and the proud mom of Kameron, her two favorite humans.

Cindy Schwerdtfeger is a wife, mom (two grown kids, a son-in-love, and a daughter-in-love), and a grandma of two. She leads a women's Bible study and is a Manager of Information Services. She will complete graduate school for IT Management soon and hopes to write more with all her 'free' time.

Camie Treptau and her family have served at VCBC in one form or another for over 50 combined years. Although camp presents challenges each year, Camie trusts that the Lord ministers through her family and the camp. She loves Jesus, her husband, her kids, and so many amazing friends and family who are such a blessing.

Bri Simpson is wife to Logan, furmom to Carson, and loves gathering as many people as possible in her tiny apartment in Dallas, Texas She worked at Village Creek for about five years and still sings camp songs whenever it's socially appropriate (and sometimes when it's not).

Austin Walker loves Jesus, his wife Calli, and his three kids Emerson, Silas, & Scarlett. He also is the Campus Pastor at @iamembrace – St. Croix Campus, in Lakeland, MN, and is the founder of @YLSummit, an organization created to reach the next generation for Jesus by loving the youth worker in their community. He loves camping, hunting, and going on vacation with his wife in his free time! In order to connect with him, email him: austin.walker@iamembrace.com

Jen Woyke lives in the Minneapolis area with her husband of 20 years and their three children. She serves in many capacities in the Christian education arena as she is passionate about church history, hymnology, and the Word. Her first trip to Village Creek Bible Camp was over 15 years ago, and she's been going back ever since!

About Village Creek Bible Camp

Since its first family camp over Memorial Day weekend in 1972, Village Creek Bible Camp has offered a variety of activities on its property. Summer camps for young people, family camps, and retreats throughout the year encourage, inspire, and challenge people of all ages in their relationship with God through Jesus Christ.

With something for everyone of every age (horses, adventure-style programming including a zip-line and ropes' course, a lake, hiking trails, crafts, an indoor gymnasium, and more), Village Creek Bible Camp provides quiet times for personal reflection, activities for fellowship and discipleship, and spiritual food from speakers to help those in attendance to find a relationship with God through Jesus Christ or to grow closer and deeper in their existing faith.

All of the contributors to this book have a connection to Village Creek Bible Camp. Many have been campers (child, youth, adult, or family) – some for only a few years while others have been involved for decades. Several have served as staff, speakers, or volunteers. All have a fondness in their heart and a gratitude for the camp and what it has done, is doing, and will do in the lives of children, adults, and families.

For more information about the camp, its programming, and ways for you to contribute to its ministries, please go to the following website: www.villagecreek.net.

123

fifty devotions to encourage and inspire

Published in June, 2015
Written by authors connected to VCBC (villagecreek.net)
Available for order online via many outlets

Good one

page 19, 20
" 27
29 *
39 *
43 *
45 *
81 Cindy

Made in the USA
Lexington, KY
18 April 2016